AF632289

INTRODUCING
TELEMEDICINE

APPLICATION • CHALLENGES • NEEDS & BENEFITS
• COMPONENTS & INFRASTRUCTURE

INTRODUCING
TELEMEDICINE

APPLICATION • CHALLENGES • NEEDS & BENEFITS • COMPONENTS & INFRASTRUCTURE

B.D. GUPTA
MD, FRCR (London)
Adviser
Telemedicine Technology Project,
Post-Graduate Institute of Medical Education
& Research (PGIMER), Chandigarh

DEEP & DEEP PUBLICATIONS PVT. LTD.
F-159, Rajouri Garden, New Delhi-110027

INTRODUCING TELEMEDICINE

ISBN 81-7629-479-9

© 2004 B.D. GUPTA

All rights reserved with the Publisher, including the right to translate or to reproduce this book or parts thereof except for brief quotations in critical articles or reviews.

Typeset by ASHISH TECHNOGRAPHICS,
3190, Mohindra Park, Shakur Basti, Delhi-110034.

Printed in India at ELEGANT PRINTERS,
A-38/2, Mayapuri, Phase-I, New Delhi-110 064.

Published by DEEP & DEEP PUBLICATIONS PVT. LTD.,
F-159, Rajouri Garden, New Delhi - 110 027
Phones : 25435369, 25440916
E-mails : ddpbooks@yahoo.co.in • deep98@del3.vsnl.net.in
Showroom :
2/13, Ansari Road, Daryaganj, New Delhi -110 002 • Telefax : 23245122

Contents

Foreword

The two relatively recent developments—rather revolutions—Information Technology and unfolding of Human Genome—are likely to speed up man's march more than any other discoveries/inventions the world has seen hitherto. The IT has resulted in tremendous spurt in communication network resulting in shrinkage of the world to a few minutes in terms of time. Any information can travel to any part of the world within no time. The revelations from the unfolding of human genome are likely to make medical practice and our beliefs upside down.

Telemedicine in clinical practice is a new concept to India while it has been in practice in the developed world for quite sometime where it is also culturally accepted. We have a situation where a patient irrespective of the distance he/she is located, can get almost instant specialist/superspecialist advice for his/her ailment which facility hitherto was available only to those living in metropolitan cities. In the absence of availability of proper guidance from a specialist, we have lost many precious lives. The importance of Telemedicine will be appreciated only when its benefits trickle down to our remote rural and semi-urban areas where 80 percent of our population lives. It is doubtful whether there is any other single development, which will allow social justice in our Health Care Programme, if the technology is implemented properly. The technology helps us make full use of the specialist/superspecialist services available for bringing solace to millions of people living in semi-urban and rural areas.

This book "Introducing Telemedicine" by Prof. B.D.

Gupta is a comprehensive publication explaining all the aspects of the Technology—its history, its advantages, its status in the developed countries, its status in India, its limitations, its requirements for being introduced at medical college, district and primary health-care levels, "Live", "Store & Forward" concepts etc. Prof. Gupta has put in extensive efforts studying many publications on the subject, witnessing practical demonstrations and indulging in personal communication with many stalwarts world over. Also he was the Coordinator of the project, when the Technology was put to use in India during the last Maha Kumbh Mela at Allahabad. While Telemedicine has a key role in patient care, it also plays an equally important role in medical education and Continuing Medical Education. It can eliminate, in a big way, the inhibition of physicians to serve in rural areas, minimizing their feeling of isolation because it enables them to consult their seniors on the lines of almost a face-to-face discussion.

I compliment the efforts of Prof. B.D. Gupta, an Emeritus Professor of PGIMER, Chandigarh, whose primary interest is Oncology with specialisation in Radiotherapy. Telemedicine is his newly acquired interest and he has done commendable work in this field as well within a short span. The efforts and the seminal input he made resulted in the sanction of a National Project entitled "Telemedicine Technology for Optimising Medical Resources" by the Govt. of India, Dept. of Electronics (subsequently re-christened as Dept. of Information Technology) with aims and objectives, to begin with: to provide networking among the three premier national medical institutions in the country, namely AIIMS, New Delhi, SGPGI, Lucknow and PGI, Chandigarh, and then to extend the facilities to the state-level medical institutions, district hospitals and ultimately to the primary health-care centres, in a phased manner.

My recommendation to the Central and State Governments is that you have a ready reckoner here should you care to introduce Telemedicine so that the benefits trickle down to the vast population living in rural India who are deprived of the modern specialist/superspecialist advice and care. Through Telemedicine, you can use the vast resources of our medical specialists in the country in clinical practice of medicine.

I congratulate Prof. B.D. Gupta and I am sure his efforts will fructify sooner than later in taking Telemedicine Technology to the remote areas and rural masses, which is the ultimate goal.

DR. S.K. SHARMA, MS, MCh
Director,
Postgraduate Institute of Medical
Education & Research, Chandigarh

Preface

Today, the medical field in India is faced with growing public as well as government demands for reform against the background of high cost involving quality health care and inability of the medical specialists to provide adequate health services to a large population especially in rural and remote areas. In response to government proposals and public needs, several health care institutions have now included on their agenda development of medical technologies to improve health care communications. Telemedicine is the term used to describe various technological developments and their application in clinical practice of Medicine. These emerging technologies, we hope, would revolutionize health care services and vastly improve the quality and quantity in medical care. Telemedicine is generally known as the use of telecommunications and computer technologies with medical expertise to facilitate health care delivery to remote patients. Telemedicine, in fact, is the practice of diagnosis, consultation and treatment of patients by tele-communication between physicians and specialists, finally, the benefits going to distant patients. Specifically, telemedicine is a 2-way audio and video communication network that allows hospitals and their physicians and specialists in the field of Medicine access to medical technological resources via telephone lines, Integrated Services Digital Network (ISDN) lines and/or satellite linkups. The specific applications of Telemedicine include:

1. Electronic management and transfer of patient information,

2. Image compression for efficient storage and retrieval of image data,
3. Image processing for diagnostic purposes, and
4. Tele-conferencing for professional consultation, education and training.

There is no doubt that the use of Telemedicine and its interactive medical technology continue to grow and many institutions, hospitals and clinics, are utilising the newer developments in Telemedicine application. However, there are a number of obstacles to the widespread implementation of the Telemedicine application in clinical practice. First, Physician's resistance to the use of new technology in patient care continues to impede Telemedicine use. Many physicians and specialists are uncomfortable with computer and its application. One physician remarked in response to the use of computer technology in Medicine "You don't put that computer on my desk. I have practised for forty years without it, and I do not need it now". No doubt, many doctors may want to use computer application but may not have enough time to learn and use the technology. This is particularly common in isolated areas where only a few physicians serve a large area. It has also been observed and reported that some of the doctors are reluctant to consult any outside physician in patient care programme. There is no doubt that Telemedicine can provide access to areas that are underserved or unserved. It can improve access to speciality care and reduce commuting time and cost for rural and semi-urban patients. It can provide greater interaction facilities between physicians to physicians and physicians to specialists, thus reducing physicians' isolation (a common occurrence in rural and semi-urban communities). Continuing Medical Education will become easier and most cost-efficient. We must understand that Telemedicine use can improve the quality of health care through more timely diagnosis and treatment of patients.

In short, Telemedicine is an emerging field that can have profound social impact on the delivery and quality of medical care. Within this context and to answer several questions and queries in the minds of medical and technical professionals, the author has embarked upon writing the present Handbook. We hope this will provide an insight to the readers and incentives for establishment of Telemedicine Technology programme in many more centres and hospitals and clinics.

The Health and Biotechnology Division of the Ministry of Information Technology, Government of India, has taken an initiative in providing support to introduce Telemedicine in India and define the role of Information Technology and Computer application in Medicine. The main aims and objectives are to extend and redefine the entire practice of health care utilising Telemedicine information technology as a welfare measure in our country. We can utilise the vast resources of medical professionals, specialists and super-specialists in the country for effective improvement and efficiency in diagnosis and treatment of our patients.

This Handbook aims to support in sensitizing the Government and many more private organisations to come forward to establish facilities for utilising telemedicine application in their clinical practice. I am sure Telemedicine will be the next big wave to inundate the practice of Medicine. The combined synergy of low cost computing power, improving telecommunication facilities (including the internet) and advances in clinical information sciences will transform how medicine is practised. Perhaps the medical profession needs help to formulate the strategic plans in health care sector. You have to be ready to prototype a telemedicine application and you need information on the latest technology in this field. It is the intention that the clinicians should get the acquisition of telemedicine application in their routine programme. I have found that most of the existing telemedicine literature focuses on Tele-radiology, Tele-pathology and Tele-dermatology and many other specialities are being investigated. We are sure that building on the foundation of Information Technology, Telemedicine application has been and continues to be developed for use across the full gamut of health care practice.

I sincerely hope that the Handbook will give information that perhaps is urgently needed to our physicians and surgeons to understand the basic concept of Telemedicine technology and its application in clinical medicine.

Chandigarh B.D. GUPTA

Acknowledgements

At the outset the author wishes to express his gratitude to the Ministry of Information Technology (Health and Bio-Technology Division), Government of India, for according approval and sponsoring the Project entitled "Development of Telemedicine Technology for Optimising Medical Resources in India". The Project is unique in the sense, it aims at introducing a new technology in clinical application of Medicine and extending quality health care facilities to each and every citizen. Telemedicine application in Health Care is a new phenomenon and it is our aim to redefine the entire practice utilising Telemedicine and Information Technology as a vehicle to improve efficiency in diagnosis and treatment. The Project will introduce telemedicine in India and develop a strategy in computer application for improvement in health care sector.

The author sincerely acknowledge the support and infrastructure provided by the authorities of Postgraduate Institute of Medical Education & Research, Chandigarh — especially the then Director Prof. B.K. Sharma and the present Director Prof. S.K. Sharma. They have given the required thrust in the implementation of Tele-medicine application as a National venture.

The Directors of the other two premier medical institutions who are participating as principal investigators in the Project: Prof. P.K. Dave of All India Institute of Medical Sciences, New Delhi and Prof. M. Bhandari, Director of Sanjay

Gandhi Post-Graduate Institute of Medical Sciences, Lucknow, deserve great appreciation for readily agreeing to join the National movement and for giving their full support in the introduction of Telemedicine Technology as a joint programme.

The author is sincerely grateful to Dr R.S. Khandpur, Director CEDTI, SAS Nagar, Mohali, and to Dr. R.K. Arora, Director, CDAC, Pune, for gladly accepting to be Principal Investigators and leaders in the joint proposal for development of Telemedicine Technology as a National Project. These two institutions are nationally and internationally reputed for electronic design and computer application. Many of the scientists working in these institutions are also actively involved in the Project and they are working whole-heartedly and literally round-the-clock to make the project a success story. To name a few: Dr A.M. Karnik and Shri Devashish Pandya of CDAC, Pune and Shri Sanjay Sood of CEDTI, SAS Nagar. Both the Institutes have developed a System for Patient Information and Electronic Patient Format in a record time. We will be soon incorporating the System in the networking of the three user medical institutions. These institutions have many achievements and credits in their respective fields and we are glad that these scientists are working right under the leadership of their Directors to support the implementation of Telemedicine Technology in clinical practice. We need their continued support.

The Investigators in the Project, Dr. Sudha Suri, Prof. and Head of Radiodiagnosis and Prof. Kusum Joshi, Prof. of Histopathology from PGIMER, Chandigarh; Dr. K.K. Talwar, Prof. of Cardiology, Shri R.S. Tyagi and Dr. Arvind from AIIMS, New Delhi, and Dr. Ratni Gujral, Prof. and Head of Radiology and Dr. S.K. Mishra, Prof. of Endocrine Surgery from SGPGIMS, Lucknow deserve a special mention for their candid co-operation and help in the development of Telemedicine Technology in their specialities and the thrust areas identified in the project : Tele-Radiology, Tele-Pathology and Tele-Cardiology which have been taken up on priority. We need their continued support and co-operation for the implementation of the project.

The author sincerely feels it is a matter of pride to acknowledge the candid support and contribution of late Shri S. Mukhopadhyay, Adviser and Shri S.R. Das, Senior Director of the Health and Bio-Technology Division of Ministry of Information Technology, Govt. of India. Without their interest and support it would not have been possible to undertake and establish the relatively new Technology in India. Presently Dr. U.P. Phadke, Adviser and Sh. K.S.K. Sai, Senior Director in the Ministry of Information Technology, Govt. of India, are giving the necessary support and are taking interest in the development of Telemedicine Application. We do need their continued help in establishing the Telemedicine facilities firmly and also to bring more and more areas under Telemedicine programme. It is our wish to continue the research and development in this field and also to make efforts to translate the benefits of Telemedicine Technology for the welfare of our patients. Shri J.S. Maini, Formerly Joint Secretary and Financial Adviser, Ministry of Information Technology, Govt. of India, deserves our thanks for the encouragement and support in the design of the project and its implementation. We take this opportunity to express our gratitude to him.

I wish to acknowledge that I have adopted three tables from the book "A Telemedicine Primer: Understanding the Issues" written by Dr. Jim Reid and have included these in the present publication with the necessary modifications as per our requirements. I also wish to acknowledge the information gathered from World Wide Web (www) sites through Internet while preparing the brief history of Telemedicine in the other countries, in general, and in India, in particular. In addition, the author has also consulted some of his friends and professional colleagues for seeking their views on correctness of the information included in the book. However, in view of paucity of time and space, their names could not be included here, but we wish to sincerely acknowledge that their views and suggestions have been of immense help to me. Last but not the least I wish to extend thanks to Mrs. Anjna Kathuria and Mr. Lalit M. Aggarwal for their valuable typing work.

We wish the present publication will encourage the medical and technical personnel to make Telemedicine a possibility in their medical practice. This is a first step towards getting a textbook on the subject for those who may choose to specialise in Telemedicine as a vocation. I would also like to initiate a journal on Telemedicine and for this purpose I request our colleagues to contribute useful material purely dedicated to the subject. We will try to organise a workshop as and when the funds are available.

A time has come when Telemedicine applications may have to be included in the curriculum at various levels of medical education. I must point out that with so much national indulgence in Information Technology, we should seriously consider providing well-laid infrastructure in every medical and research centre in India for practicing Telemedicine.

Chandigarh B.D. GUPTA

1

CHAPTER

Introduction to Telemedicine

Tele-medicine has great potential and will certainly have a significant role on the future of Medicine than any other modality in the twenty-first century.

1. In the remote areas it can bring high quality medical care where almost none is available at present.
2. It can provide a lifeline to medical expertise and can provide the urgently needed health care in primary and community health as well as secondary care hospitals in the country.

The technology can universalise and standardise the quality of medical care in the developing countries, especially in India where remote areas are still not easily accessible.

Telemedicine in its true sense is the transmission of medical information in the form of audio, video, text and images of patients from one location to another, using telecommunication channels. The main communication is between two or more clinics, hospitals, institutions and health centres, within a country or outside, for consultation, advice and opinion. Telemedicine also means transfer of expertise from one point to another and it is the fastest means of communication for consultation for improvement and efficiency in diagnosis and treatment. In addition, high quality medical services of specialists and super-specialists can be readily available using telecommunication and computer technology.

The most important aspect of telemedicine is the digital convergence of medical records, charts, X-rays, histopathology slides and medical procedures (including lab. tests) conducted on the patients. This is precisely known as Electronic Patient Record (EPR) in Telemedicine practice. Modern computer application and utilisation of powerful tele-communication systems have created a revolution in that Telemedicine can be practised as "Real Time" and/or "Store and Forward" multimedia information transfer in patient care, medical education and research. Real time (synchronous) interactive video conferencing and thereby direct discussion with experts at a distance is becoming a reality. The greatest beneficiary is the community situated in remote areas. We have the means available for electronic transmission of audio, video, text and image data of patients anywhere and at anytime. We can practice telemedicine as "Real Time" (synchronous interactive video-conferencing) and/or "Store and Forward" format based on patient data and record for further consultation, information and advice. Medicine can now extend its reach, regardless of physical distance through real time or near real time using two-way transmission of information between places of lesser and/or greater medical capabilities and expertise. Telemedicine will revolutionize the current clinical medical practice and we can extend instant medical support to a remote or geographically dispersed population in the near future.

3. In the Western and developed countries, clinical medicine is reaching even into the home-care telemedical services and is evolving itself as an effective and efficient tool even for long-term care of the elderly and chronically ill patients.

The most promising and established telemedicine application in the developed countries is also practised as on-line and off-line telemedicine technology with special reference to tele-radiology, tele-pathology, tele-dermatology, tele-cardiology and, recently, tele-psychiatry. It has been reported that interactive tele-health services will be routinely available in those countries and facilities may extend into the "drawing room" of the patient as that of tele-banking where the customer has access to his/her bank account.

It is essential to know that health care facilities contribute substantially to the social and economic foundations of our rural and semi-urban communities. Medical care, especially its quality, is the greatest challenge in the health care delivery system in India. The care is most unequally distributed and it is a great challenge to the government and the professionals in the country. The rural communities also require the same 24-hour health care service as the urban communities. Further, the doctors posted in rural and semi-urban primary and secondary care hospitals are professionally isolated. They do not have the support and company of their colleagues. They do not have the benefits of discussions and interaction, particularly on complex problems of patients, with their colleagues which are readily available in urban and, more so, in metropolitan and large cities. The professional isolation is really a major factor in keeping the doctors away from rural areas where the conditions/facilities available are not attractive. They have no professional satisfaction in their practice. This has even resulted in the closure of many primary and community centres and hospitals in the country or they have become defunct in the absence of medical professionals.

Telemedicine technology, through the available telecommunication links, can extend its helping hand to the patient (and to the professionals as well) in the management of their illnesses by eliminating the delay in diagnosis and treatment and providing quality health care.

One of its important applications is in Continuing

Medical Education (CME) programme. This is a useful means for medical, nursing and para-medical professionals as well as for those undergoing internship. Apart from the other areas, Telemedicine technology can be utilised to harness the vast resources of medical professionals and specialists in the region, in particular, and the country, in general, for CME programmes. The required Software and Hardware are now available for transmission of audio, video and text via Telecommunication lines. (This aspect will be discussed in detail in a following Chapter). In one of their publications, Hartman and Moore (1992) reported that 75 per cent of physicians, 92 per cent of nurses and 88 per cent of supporting health care workers, who participated in telemedicine CME Programme, admitted having gained considerably in their professional activities and in updating their knowledge of modern technology. These authors also stressed that professional isolation is one of the major factors in keeping the health personnel away from remote areas. Telemedicine practice in rural areas has been proved to be the most useful in attracting the health care workers to work there because they are not deprived of contact with their counterparts in the urban areas. They further observed that tele-CME programmes have, in fact, infused in them a closer sense of contact with their senior colleagues. Williams and Moore (1995) further reported that access to Continuing Education Programme has increased manifold the "Real Time" interaction in Telemedicine practice. It was especially observed that it has given greater professional satisfaction among the physicians and it was the most cost-efficient means of education in Medicine. It has also ushered in a new era in serving the professional interests of the physicians located in primary and secondary health care centres located in remote areas.

Telemedicine can provide high quality clinically relevant medical updates and access to modern technology in diagnosis and treatment through educational programmes.

The cost of the equipment is not enormous in view of the corresponding facilities and benefits likely to derive. The most common requirement is a desktop computer with a video camera system with or without zoom facilities. The system can work on telephone lines in remote areas if ISDN lines are not available. The facilities can also be extended to medical administrative functions for administration of health care centres located in remote areas.

The armed forces in the USA have taken an active role in the utilisation of Telemedicine Technologies and in the use of interactive video conferencing for their forward areas in their own country and in other countries where the forces are stationed. They have a wide area network for providing quality care to their military personnel who need specialised and super-specialised care which is not readily available at their site of posting and in forward areas. They have also designed several research activities in preventive medicine, in the study of hypertension and diabetes and mental health care including psychiatry. We can take up a similar lead in Telemedicine application for our Army Medical Services. In India, there is ample scope in telemedicine application in forward areas and base hospitals. They can be connected with command and speciality hospitals for consultation and advice. In situations like war, the technology can provide greater and better service for the injured personnel to save their lives.

WHAT IS TELEMEDICINE?

Telemedicine, like many emerging technologies, has no universally accepted definition despite the fact that Telemedicine has been in clinical practice for more than forty years. In simple terminology, Telemedicine is the use of electronic communication networks for transmission of physical and clinical information and patient data related to diagnosis and treatment of medical conditions. In other words, telemedicine is the use of telecommunication for medical diagnosis and patient care. Thus, broadly defined, it is the use of communication technology for health care services and safely can be defined as a 2-way audio and video communication network that gives clinics, hospitals and their doctors access to medical and technological resources via communication channels using telephone lines, satellite linkups and other communication media. On a review of the available literature, a variety of telemedicine definitions were found. Goldberg in 1995 defined 'Telemedicine as the delivery of care to the patients anywhere in the world by combining communication technology with medical expertise'. In the same year, Scannel *et al.* described that 'telemedicine is the use of telecommunication for medical diagnosis and patient care'. Sund and Rinde (1995) gave a new thought that "Telemedicine is the practice of diagnosis, consultation and treatment between physicians and distant patients, through the use of special telephone lines and computers that transmit data for remote television viewing, electronic stethoscope and diagnostic instruments equipped with miniature video camera for sophisticated diagnosis and medical treatment at distance." The Telemedicine Programme, Information Technology Services and Research Division of the University of Kansas Medical Centre, USA (1995) has described that Telemedicine is "The use of telecommunication technology to enable medical care and education over a distance." Reif (1996) in his book, "A Telemedicine Primer—Understanding the Issue" defines "Telemedicine is the use of Advanced Telecommunication Technology to exchange health information and to provide health services across geographical, time, social and cultural barriers."

Telemedicine is an easily understood concept. It was developed to provide greater quality health care to people more efficiently and effectively. Telemedicine, as stated earlier, is the transformation of electronic medical data in the form of high resolution images, sounds, live-video and records through a variety of telecommunication technology such as ordinary telephone lines, ISDN lines (more frequently) or full T-1, ATM, the internet and satellites. Telemedicine has the capability to improve the delivery of health care by providing a wide-range of services to individuals and communities both urban and rural. Further Telemedicine can retain health professionals in the rural areas by providing ongoing training in collaboration with health professionals in the region and the country as well. Telemedicine allows medical and paramedical professionals to have access to the expertise of a specialist for patient care and management programme. There is a greater ease with which consultations can be obtained. It must be understood right at the initial stage that Telemedicine does not replace the need for face-to-face consultation. The patient who needs special procedures and diagnostic tests will still have to come to higher medical centres and hospitals. However, the process of making a decision as to whether a patient needs a particular procedure can often be done by using tele-consultation and distant advice. The follow-up care and integration with the primary care physician can be done by Telemedicine Technology.

The FDA (The Food and Drug Administration, USA), an authority which regulates the medical field as well, define Telemedicine as "The delivery and provision of health care and consultative services to individual patients and the transmission of information related to care, over distance, using telecommunication technologies and incorporating:

1. Direct clinical, preventive, diagnostic and therapeutic services and treatment,
2. consultative and follow-up services,
3. remote monitoring of patients,
4. rehabilitative services, or
5. patient education."

2

CHAPTER

Telemedicine—A Brief History

Telemedicine, right at the beginning of the twenty-first century, may become one of the important disciplines to deliver health care to our people, especially those living in remote and distant areas. The development of telemedicine is one of the most important and exciting examples of technology and its ability to transform and improve health care. The clinical practice of Telemedicine has become possible due to improvement in telecommunication system and its capacity to transmit audio, video and text (including images) of the patient and interactive video application in patient care.

The history of Telemedicine can be traced back to 1959 when psychiatrists at the University of Nebraska School of Medicine (USA) used a microwave video link for consultation on their patients with health professionals at the State Mental Hospital located over a hundred miles away. In the early part of 1960, the National Aeronautic Space Administration (NASA), USA, developed a medical communication system with Red Indian reservation area in Arizona to provide health care over a large distance. This is the beginning of health care programme through Telemedicine, in the United States and the first of its kind with the interest of NASA. In 1968, a group of doctors at the Mass General Hospital in Boston (USA) had established a video network to examine the emergency patients at Logan International Airport (Boston), and to overcome the traffic jams that often prevented the travel via the connecting tunnel under Boston Harbour. The actual practice of Telemedicine to the community began in 1980s with several projects funded by several agencies in the United States of America to undertake interactive video networking between rural and urban health system. The patients in remote communities were examined by a specialist situated at medical centres at a distance. The rural health professionals have also used the same facilities for Continuing Education Programme and administrative meetings with distant colleagues. It was reported in the earlier literature that the first generation telemedicine had certainly eliminated one significant barrier, i.e., accessibility for the patient and professionals situated in a remote and distant area. However, in those days it was more costly and time-consuming than the traditional face-to-face care and consultation. It was a great beginning when interactive video linkages created a new possibility for doctor-patient and doctor specialist interaction. These movements in Telemedicine were however, not enough and not culturally acceptable for the fear that the very foundation of health care practice may be shaken.

The real revolution in telemedicine practice started when tele-communications and computers converged during the last decade of the twentieth century, i.e., the beginning of 1990s. The clinicians and the entrepreneurs with more vision and ideas quickly began to see the transformable power of the internet, the world wide web (www) and the related technology of digital photography and its application. We can call the development "A second generation telemedicine" which was started somewhere in the middle of 1990s when the application became more practical, time-saving and cost effective. The use of telemedicine began with Tele-radiology and Tele-dermatology as an emerging application in clinical practice. A digitized photograph of skin lesions was taken, at the patient's convenience, and sent over the internet to a dermatologist for review at a later time by specialists and super-specialists for their consultation and advice. Similarly, CT and MRI images and scans were sent for downloading to a specialist situated at a distance for his interpretation for definite diagnosis and advice. Home-bound patients or people at work in their offices began using new devices to send their results of laboratory tests to a doctor's office and to their on-line medical record for monitoring of their illnesses. It is also reported that the *Wall Street Journal* has had regularly covered the evolution of Telemedicine business and published stories with headings like "Taking Care of Patients: New High-tech Links can offer Some Relief" and "A doctor, 700 patients, and the net: Inventing the virtual house call," published on January 17, 2000.

The third generation of Telemedicine may have begun with the development of equipment and accessories connected with digital technology in the form of electronic stethoscope, ophthalmoscope and so on, and the products used in Teleradiology and Telepathology, mainly the scanners and video cameras. You can say that Telemedicine has just started as a real clinical practice. The definition of Telemedicine will continue to expand and we should all expect many surprises. There are several different names/terms/terminologies attached to this new technology and the new way of health care and clinical practice: the network medicine, tele-health, digital medicine, distributed health care and so on have been found in the literature specially in the current use of telemedicine practice. Telehealth, the most common alternative to Telemedicine, is used especially to differentiate health care from medical care. This is to draw a definition between a comprehensive view and more focused model of medical doctors. The convergence of telecommunications and computers will change the future for everyone from the new age healer to medical sub-specialists. The use of telemedicine in this form reflects the most common practice and implies no disrespect to alternative terminology. The discipline that is known today "Telemedicine" should not mean a special name when computer networks and telecommunications system are fully integrated with the very fabric of medicine. Telemedicine will become synonymous with health care over the coming years and we hope the special terminology will disappear gradually.

In the early days, during the end of 1980s and beginning of 1990s, a mini-television studio was required for telemedicine practice. There was a huge console with full of electronic equipment at each end of the clinical sites. There was also a necessity that at both the specialist and patient/ referral end; they (doctor and patient) need to be present in their respective places at the appointed time. There was also a requirement for computer and video technicians to be involved at both sites. The process was certainly more cumbersome, expensive and time-consuming as compared with the traditional doctor-patient visit. In due course, however, most of the equipments were miniaturized and also became portable. Even the typical units at the referring physician end and at the receiving end need not be similar. They simply comprise a digital monitor with computer and a video camera. This can be installed on the top of a table and can be plugged into a regular telephone line and/or ISDN lines whichever available. It does not require the actual presence of a computer specialist and a technician. Recently, a complete home telemedicine kit which includes a video camera and some of the digital peripherals to record the vital signs has been introduced which can be conveniently used in home care telemedicine programme.

A new technology is also emerging in the form of next generation wireless telephone, better known as "personal communication system" or PCS where a considerable amount of medical information can be exchanged between both the ends, i.e., patient or referring physician and the specialist. Palm-top computers, also known as personal digital assistance or PDA, are already linked with health professionals to transmit the medical records and health planned data in some of the developed countries. The technology of convergence of POS and PAD will certainly permit physicians, nurses and other health professionals to review data, previously provided by the patients from their homes, make diagnosis and order treatment whenever and wherever they want. Perhaps this is the hope that Telemedicine of the twenty-first century holds.

We are nearing the point that Telemedicine and all that it promised in the April 1924 issue of "Radio News" where the implication demonstrated a "Radio Doctor" at work. It demonstrated a great future for radio as a vehicle for "Radio Doctor." The forerunner of modern telemedicine practitioner. The device which they have published in their News Bulletin provided a remote means of obtaining the patient's pulse rate, temperature and heart sound. It also allowed the doctor to write prescription remotely and had a 2-way visual communication between the patient and the physician. The following picture depicts the era and "crystal sets" and horn speakers when commercial broadcasting was only four years old in 1924 (with the first broadcasting coming from KDKA in Pittsburgh, USA in 1920.

FIG. 1

Radio Doctor Year, 1924

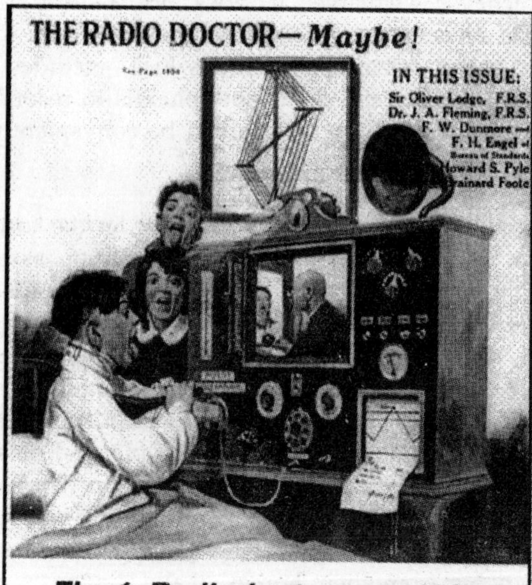

Fig. 1 Radiodoctor year 1924

THE INDIAN SCENE

Today, the medical field is faced with growing public and government demands for reforms. In response to public needs and government proposals, health care institutions in government and private sector are adopting and developing medical technology in diagnosis and treatment and extending their services to semi-urban and rural areas. Telemedicine is one of the new and emerging disciplines, a result of the ongoing Information Technology revolution, where telecommunications and computer application with medical expertise available in our country can support health care delivery to our people and especially in the improvement in practice of diagnosis, consultation and treatment between physicians and patients located at distant places. There have been attempts and advancements for telemedicine mediated services in our hospitals and institutions in India. However, the development and establishment of telemedicine are located in metropolitan and large cities and are used for consultation and opinion from one hospital to another. The technology is also extended for consultation from specialists in other countries in a limited area of medical specialists.

The then Department of Electronics, Govt. of India (now the Ministry of Information Technology) has approved a project "Telemedicine Technology for Optimising Medical Resources" with connectivity among the three premier institutions in the country, namely: All India Institute of Medical Sciences, New Delhi; Post-graduate Institute of Medical Education & Research, Chandigarh; and Sanjay Gandhi Post-graduate Institute of Medical Sciences, Lucknow. This project was approved in 1998 and started functioning from April 1999. The main thrust areas, to begin with, are: Tele-radiology and Tele-pathology for exchange and transmission of images for discussion, education and opinion. The transmission of data is to be carried out with ISDN lines. In addition, the facilities for real-time video conferencing were also to be established for medical education and live demonstration of the ongoing programme of interest, seminars and conferences between the three institutions. The project has initiated its programme and is in the establishment phase where medical peripherals are under installation. The other participating institutions in the project are Centre for Electronic Design and Technology, SAS Nagar and the Centre for Development of Advanced Computing, Pune. They are working very actively and developing the necessary software and to provide essential ingredient and interfaces in the project. A great deal of work is completed in Telemedicine Application for the project.

A Medical Computer Society was established in Chennai at the end of 1998 with the main idea and objective of identifying the ongoing Telemedicine developments especially in the use of electronic mail and internet for medical practice. The Society is providing a catalytic role between the industry and the physician and supporting internet access in health information. The members of the Society are also involved in the establishment of a database describing extremely rare diseases in India and accumulation of medical statistics to be used by medical and allied professionals.

The Gujarat Narmada Fertilizer Corporation (GNFC) in Ahmedabad has established a Medical Information Division in association with KBC group under leadership of Shri Ragesh Shah. They have developed an extremely useful Telemedicine System which can be connected with telephone lines as well as ISDN lines. The system is complete and has facilities for transmission of data in the form of audio-video, images and texts. The system can be used as a Real-Time and Store and Forward format between clinics, hospitals and physicians for exchange of information and for obtaining their opinion and advice. This can also be utilised between physicians, and physicians and patients. The efforts of this Group are encouraging in that the system is ready for use in clinical practice with minimal input.

The Indian Institute of Technology, Kharagpur, has developed a Telemedicine system where patient data including images can be transferred via telephone lines between one station and another. The system can be utilised in primary and secondary care programmes with direct communication between medical college hospitals and major hospitals.

There are several private institutions in the country which are directly and indirectly involved in Telemedicine practice. The Apollo hospitals group is the one organisation which is in the process of developing Telemedicine Technology and it has a future programme for interconnectivity with their hospitals located at different places in the country. Hyderabad is the one city which has also planned a Virtual University for exchange of health information and use of telemedicine technology in the health care delivery. The main thrust area of the proposed university is to utilise the digital revolution and establish an affordable telemedicine work station in every hospital and at every physician's workplace to make Medicine high quality and cost-effective in health care programme to every patient. They have also a programme to provide medical informatics and database for medical professionals which is greatly lacking in this country.

There are a few telemedicine technology centres for telemedicine consultation and a live interactive video conferencing with overseas consultants for opinion and advice. This is a purely private adventure where patient data are put into an electronic medical folder and transmitted by the centre to the consultant overseas. These centres have been functioning in Mumbai, Delhi and Chennai. However, they have a low key profile and their impact is yet to be felt in Telemedicine practice in the country.

Recently, the Ministry of Health and Family Welfare, Govt. of India, has set-up a Committee on the use of Information Technology in Medical Education and Health Sciences. The main objective is to define the status and use of Information Technology in medical and dental education in the country. The Committee is also to formulate a policy framework and to advise a suitable strategy for introduction of IT in medical education and in Continuing Medical Education to medical, nursing and paramedical personnel. The Ministry of Health is very keen to establish networking among medical colleges and major medical institutions in the country to utilise the vast resources of medical specialists for improvement in health care delivery. This is an encouraging gesture of the Ministry of Health to establish a Department or Division in Information Technology in each and every medical college in the country.

The Armed Forces Medical Services have also plan to develop networking between their field hospitals, base hospitals and command hospitals with their existing telemedicine link for Real Time video conferencing as well as Store and Forward concept of transmission of their medical data. A beginning has already started with their Western Command hospital functioning in Chandimandir (near Chandigarh). The thrust area would be the extension of specialist and super-specialist services to the base and field hospitals utilising telemedicine technology.

A significant development in Telemedicine Technology is reported from Ahmedabad where online telemedicine is being practised with an ordinary telephone line as well as on ISDN channel in clinical practice. Using indigenous technology, a team headed by Mr. Ragesh Shah, Chairman of the Online Telemedicine Research Institute, Ahmedabad, developed a system which can be used to transmit online ECG, CT scan, MRI, Pathology slides and reports including Doctor's prescription and moving images. The moving images may include X-rays, sonography, angiography, 2-dimensional echo and coloured Doppler for precise diagnosis and advice for treatment. According to Mr. Shah, the system is capable to support the specialists and super specialists to gather maximum information of the patients directly and also from Doctors situated in the periphery. The specialists can even get the feel of patient's heart sound by using an electronic stethoscope which is attached to a computer and the peripheral in the community health centre. The most important innovation, according to Mr. Shah, is the Event Recorder (ER). The ER has no cords attached to it. The patient has to simply place it on his/her chest, push a button, and wait for a minute for recording the ECG. After recording, the patient or his relation has to dial the telephone number of their Doctor and place the equipment on the mouthpiece of the telephone and press the same button again. ER converts the electronic signals into audio-signals which again get converted into electronic signals on the Doctor's personal computer. The ER has an advanced technology, and was also tested on domestic flights, in moving vehicles, offices and parks and it is reported that it worked to the satisfaction of medical experts. The present author has also seen the working of Event Recorder and was greatly impressed with the development of this technology under the care of Shri Ragesh Shah. The system is a useful innovation in home-care telemedicine practice where the patient can have direct access to his/her doctor and can provide useful information and the ECG recording by using telephone lines. It has been informed that as many as fifty such systems have been installed in Gujarat itself and many more centres will be coming forward in the near future.

Dr. K. Ganapathi, an eminent neurosurgeon in Apollo Hospital, Chennai, has expressed his views during his lecture on the topic "Telemedicine—A Clinical Perspective" delivered in April 2000 in one of the meetings in Hyderabad. He discussed that the delivery of health care in India given the projected growth of Information Technology, will ensure that every citizen should have access to the appropriate specialists for medical consultation. The secondary and tertiary medical care is not uniformly available in all the suburb and urban areas he said. At the same time there are scores of urban medical specialists geographically clustered and under-employed, and not willing to be relocated due to lack of infrastructure and fear of professional isolation. He further described that with the development in the field of communication and use of computers, satellite transmission and laying of fibre optic cables in India. Telemedicine will become a reality where equal distribution of health care can be provided to a large population in most parts of the country. Dr. Ganapathi, who is also an adjunctant Professor in the School of Electronics and Communication Engineering of Annamalai University, Chennai, discussed in the same forum that in order to implement the Telemedicine Programme in India, we need:

(1) Faster transmission and better image quality for diagnosis and treatment,

(2) Medical Coordination for each speciality and formulation of ground-rules, and

(3) Technical coordination to identify the most-effective mode of data acquisition, compression, transfer and manipulation of images and graphics.

He further emphasised that we must have the following points for consideration in Telemedicine Technology programme in India:

1. A ten-year Master Plan for the whole country,
2. Promotion of telemedicine services with awareness programme,
3. Joint venture to share resources, close cooperation between academicians, industry, Government, community and funding agencies, and
4. Semi-urban and rural telemedicine to be viewed as "not-for-profit."

Profits will accrue as indirect spin-offs.

In summary, he discussed that theoretically it is easier to set-up an excellent telecommunication infrastructure in semi-urban and rural India than to place hundreds of medical specialists in these places. He further said that optic fiber cables, global satellite line system and various other methods can be used to provide health care even in remote areas in India.

An eminent cardiologist, Dr. N. Trehen of Escorts Hospital, New Delhi, presented his thoughts in the same meeting at Hyderabad that in Teleradiology the transmission of telephonic electro-cardiographic monitoring was a very convenient and an "all time available monitoring facility for establishment of patient-physician contact in the shortest possible time." It is useful in rendering instant advice for hospitalisation in emergency situations while avoiding unnecessary visits to the hospital. Dr. Trehen further informed that transmission of 2-dimensional echocardiogram and coloured Doppler flow of images from remote areas to referral centres has become possible with the use of special technology. They have established telemedicine system as early as in May, 1996 and many patients have been benefited by using the technology for the monitoring of cardiac patients in their areas. In their study, out of 3119 systematic transmissions, 2683 (86 per cent) were received for cardiac systems and 436 (14 per cent) for non-cardiac systems. In their studies, 79 per cent patients had chest pain or palpitation at the time of transmission where 21 per cent had other systems like chest discomfort, breathlessness and dizziness. They focused that the home-care telemedicine and cardiology can help in significant reduction of hospitalization of patients and what they need is only reassurance and some form of drugs dose adjustment for their treatment. Only 80 patients out of 3119 were hospitalised as emergency patients. This saved a large number of patients from the need of hospitalisation.

The Centre for Electronic Design and Technology (CEDT), SAS Nagar, Punjab, one of the collaborating institutes in National Telemedicine Technology Project, Govt. of India, under the dynamic leadership of its Director Dr. R.S. Khandpur and their scientists have designed and developed a software programme for Electronic Patient Record where all kinds of information including images and ECG recording can be digitised and stored in a computer system. The development is complete and we are in the process of developing a technology for transmission of data from one place to another using ISDN lines. The scientists in CEDT are working very closely with the Post-graduate Medical Institute, Chandigarh, and we hope to establish networking between the two and more institutions very shortly. The Centre for Development of Advanced Computing, Pune (CDAC) is developing software and technology for Telemedicine workstation for physicians to physician and patients to hospital and at physician's end. The technology is required for optimising medical resources in the country. CDAC is actively participating in the National Telemedicine Project under guidance of Dr. R.K. Arora, its Director.

This is a very prestigious project supported by the Ministry of Information Technology, Govt. of India. Very senior scientists like late Sh. S. Mukhopadhyay, Adviser to the Ministry (he was the greatest source of inspiration and also was the Chairman of Steering and Review Committee of the project. The untimely demise was a great blow to the telemedicine project and his absence is certainly felt). Sh. S.R. Das, Senior Director is also actively involved in the development. We hope that all the three participating Medical Institutions and the two Technical Institutions will be interlinked with networking programme with the existing telecommunication channels including ISDN.

3

CHAPTER

Telemedicine Application in Clinical Practice

Telemedicine is not a new discipline. It is simply a new technology where a powerful telecommunication medium and computers are used for consultation, opinion and advice. The utilisation of telemedicine network is certainly a new dimension in clinical practice for patient care and it is a great system to support the medical fraternity as well. It is imperative that the advantages of the all-pervading modern Information Technology (IT) must be incorporated into physician's practice and their education, including Continuing Medical Education. The training component is an important ingredient in the practice of telemedicine technology, particularly in facilitating relationship between the users, whether primary or secondary care physicians or tertiary care hospitals or between a physician and a consultant or a specialist. There should be a definite goal irrespective of whether "Real Time" or "Store & Forward" concept is applicable. This largely depends upon the need, the interactive medical personnel, the budget at the user-site and the availability of experts at the referral-site. There are well-defined procedures in Telemedicine application. These can be classified as follows:

I. TELE-CONSULTATION

In normal practice, the consultation is done between a patient and his/her doctor or a consultant for advice and treatment. In Tele-consultation, the patient is substituted by his/her Electronic Patient Record (EPR) which has complete information on his/her physical and clinical examinations, and other investigations, if any, along with diagnosis and differential diagnosis made by the primary or the secondary care physician(s). The programme can be extended to "Real-Time" communication where the consultant can interact with the patient, of course, in the presence and support of the local doctor.

It is essential to understand right at the beginning that there is a well-defined programme of electronic patient record for tele-consultation procedure. This includes patient's identification in terms of Registration Number, Name, Address, Age, Sex, Occupation, and other related information. It should also include the chief complaints in the form of personal, family and past history and the symptoms and signs of the patient. This is followed by physical and general examinations and all the presenting symptoms and signs pertaining to the disease. Care must be taken to define the clinical areas of diagnosis and differential diagnosis for prompt advice and opinion. There is also ample scope for specific/specialist consultation where expert advice and opinion is sought involving a particular speciality. It, however, requires additional information about the organ and site of illness, which also goes into EPR. This implies areas such as Tele-cardiology where a current ECG with at least 30 seconds to one minute heart sound and the Echo-cardiogram, if available, must form a part of the records for onward transmission. This helps the specialist at the other end to have complete evaluation of the patient record in terms of final diagnosis, opinion and advice on the correct line of treatment.

It is essential that the "Package" of information needs to be transmitted to the consultant in specific tele-consultation and tele-diagnostic programme.

The following Table shows the basic information to be provided for general as well as specific tele-consultation, which are the essential ingredients in the practice of Telemedicine technology.

TABLE I

Telemedicine Application

Data Sharing	Electronic Patient Records (EPR)
	Medical Informatics
Audio	Face to face discussion
	Transmission of live heart sounds (Electronic Stethoscope)
Video	Tele-consultation
	Medical Education and CME
	Administration
	Community Health Care Programme
Still Image	Tele-radiology
	Tele-pathology
	Tele-dermatology
Tele-consultation	Tele-radiology
	Tele-pathology
	Tele-cardiology
	Tele-psychiatry
	Tele-dermatology
	Tele-surgery

2. TELE-DIAGNOSIS

This is sharing of mostly still images by a doctor at a particular location with experts at the same hospital or at some other hospital. There is an essential requirement that there is no appreciable loss of image quality during acquisition and/or transmission. The acquisition process is a technology with hardware and software and will be described in detail in a following chapter. The display of images at the specialist's end should be precise and perfect which is, in fact, the key feature in tele-diagnosis and telemedicine practice. The communication technology should be relatively using high bandwidth where audio, video and texts are mixed into a short or multimedia model along with the images to be transmitted to the experts for interpretation, opinion and final diagnosis. The results are communicated to the referring physician or radiologist/pathologist stationed in a primary or secondary health care centre. The greatest use in tele-diagnosis is tele-radiology and tele-pathology where the images are acquired and transmitted in Store and Forward format. In recent years, tele-dermatology has also emerged a challenging field for improvement in clinical diagnosis and treatment of skin diseases.

(a) Tele-Radiology

This is electronic transmission of radiologic images from one location to another for purposes of interpretation, consultation or both. A Teleradiology system consists of an Image Acquisition Division, and an Image Display/ Interpretation by a specialist who is connected by a communication network. Image acquisition is performed by a film digitizer with tele-conversion by a conventional X-ray to digital format. There are two different techniques for film digitisation: (1) Charged Coupled Devices (CCD), (2) Laser Digitizer. The best way in contrast and spatial resolution of the images with laser technology. However, the system is more expensive and its procurement for Tele-radiology depends upon the availability of funds. In the CCD, the contrast and spatial resolution is lower than laser technology. However, in recent years, CCD performance is improving and it appears that this may be the future technology of choice being less expensive and easy to maintain.

In some of the modern hospitals, established in recent years, a "filmless" system has been developed which is known as "Computer Radiography Phosphor" where storage plates are used to obtain direct digital images, which are finally transmitted as electronic patient image. The electronic display images are identical to those available on conventional or laser printed films.

The choice of telecommunication medium for Tele-radiology depends upon the number of cases referred to for consultation, size of the hospital, an average size of the files and the activities of the hospital. The higher the bandwidth, the more rapid transmission and certainly there is a greater capacity of the network used between the end-users. In primary as well as in secondary care hospitals, where ISDN lines are not readily available, telephone lines are used for transmission of images; of course, this is slow and utmost care must be taken to see that there is no loss of image quality during transmission.

(b) Tele-Pathology

Tele-pathology is one of the fastest growing fields in telemedicine technology in the world. The most important application of tele-pathology is for consultation, opinion (second or third), quality control and certainly for educational promotion. This helps and supports in accurate diagnosis and treatment and can be life-saving for the patient. Tele-pathology is largely based on the delivery of microscopic images by the pathologist who runs them through the glass slides and observes it at different objective magnifications, looking for the best diagnostic clues that may be found in specific optical fields. The selected images thus are transferred into the computer system which is attached to a microscope through a sensitive digital static or video camera and stored for the clinical practice. This is commonly known as "Store and Forward" concept of Telemedicine Telepathology. In the practice of Store and Forward concept, the pathologist at the other end or at a distance from the referring pathologist scans images received by him and makes opinion and reports for the referring pathologist. The alternate practice of telepathology (other than Store and Forward concept) is Real Time telepathology where a robotized microscope is used for full remote movements from the other end or at a distance and makes the best choice of field selection for imaging and interpretation. The remote controlled system helps the pathologists at both the ends where they have to be present at that particular application to satisfy their observations and different objective magnifications for diagnostic clues for specific optical fields.

The Real Time tele-pathology requires high bandwidth and, in addition, certainly expensive tools for its practice, especially with a robotised microscope. The simultaneous presence of specialists at both the ends is an essential requirement for a joint collaboration programme.

FIG. 2

Real Time Tele-pathology

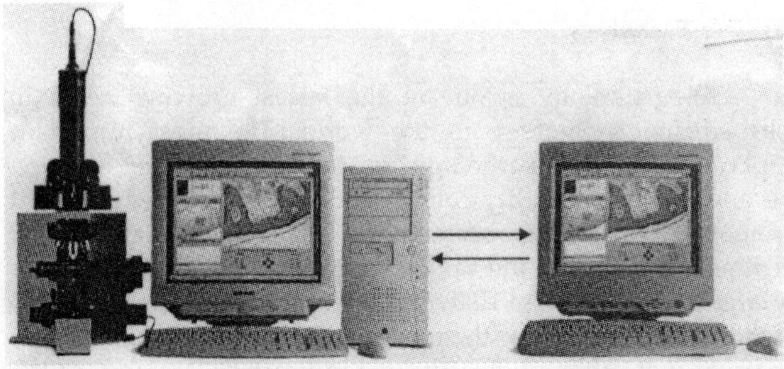

(a) Computer in the Laboratory (b) Computer at a distance

On the contrary, S&F tele-pathology is far less expensive except that it requires most sensitive and high-resolution microscope and digital camera. In addition, this can also be practised on Internet, of course, with limitations. The best way to practice telepathology is through ISDN lines, which can support major teaching hospitals and research institutions. It is essential to note that tele-pathology on the internet is largely used for connecting primary health centres and district hospitals with major teaching hospitals or a tertiary care hospital in the region or in the country. It is interesting to note that most of the internet protocols and tools necessary to implement tele-pathology are in common communication use. To enumerate: there are electronic mail with attachments and wave-related technology. Most of the studies reported have demonstrated the overall feasibility of telepathology on the internet although problems appear when dealing with specific fields and, particularly, difficult cases. It has been stated by several workers that E-mail protocols seem to be particularly suited to telemedicine since they provide direct solution for many telemedical needs especially where multimedia facilities are required. They are simple to use and can keep privacy and certainly security.

3. TELEMEDICINE INFRASTRUCTURE

(i) Image Information Acquisition (Capture) Equipment

It is a combination of hardware and software which acquires the physical and clinical information of the patient in the form of audio, video clips, texts and images. This format is known as Electronic Patient Record (EPR). This is an essential requirement for transmission of patient data from one point to another for consultation, opinion and advice (also called "end-to-end user"). The equipment can be most simple and inexpensive or complex and expensive, comparable to multimedia system used in broadcasting studios. It must be understood that in clinical application it is not the digital or video camera alone which provides the electronic information, but also the several equipment and devices used in compiling the patient medical data which are commonly known as Medical Peripherals in telemedicine technology. They are in the form of electronic stethoscope, various kinds of scopes ranging from ear scope, ophthalmoscope to other kinds of still and dynamic images-capturing devices, X-ray films and histopathology slide digitizer; a digital-capturing board within a computer or outside (known as writing pad for exchanging notes and even appending signature of the doctors), and digital devices which are routinely used during patient examination and investigation. These instruments are also called "End-User" equipment. The end-users are the physicians, nurses and telemedicine technicians who actually use the equipment to acquire patient information and images to be used for transmission.

(ii) Information

There are four kinds of information that require transmission from one point to another in telemedicine technology programmes, such as tele-consultation, tele-diagnosis and tele-health care.

(a) Audio Information

This can be described as simple spoken words or recorded voices of the patients, physicians and/or more sophisticated sound of heart and lungs. It is important to know that high quality sound transmission requires relatively a simple technology which is not expensive proposition.

(b) Graphics

These are clinical images of patients, in the form of texts, documents specially of laboratory tests, X-rays, pathology and other similar images and diagrams used in clinical medicine. This is a highly complex technology-oriented programme for acquiring patient data for transmission. This needs high resolution image display and manipulation software at the consultant's or referral hospital's end.

(c) Video

This is acquisition of Live and/or Stored electronic information. There are several types of video-capture systems available from simple still cameras to sophisticated pan tilt and zoom cameras. The camera can also move with the sound of the patient, the doctor and other staff who are involved in the patient care. This technology is commonly used in Real-Time video conferencing system.

(d) Electronic Data Information

This information comprises patient history, results of examination and other tests of the patient which require electronic conversion. The quality acquisition of this information largely depends upon the equipment used at the primary site and the software programme applied. The system, therefore, has to be comprehensive when used in Telemedicine Technology.

(iii) Implementation and Application

The technology depends upon the concept of Telemedicine practice whether Real-Time and/or Store and Forward architecture. The following points need consideration in clinical application:

(a) Data-Sharing—These include:
  - (i) Patient's records.
  - (ii) Tests' results in the form of imaging and laboratory data.

(b) Voices—of the patient and of the physician and/or of the consultant.

(c) Still images—Teleradiology, Telepathology, Teledermatology and so on.

(d) Video—used in the form of:
  - (i) Teleconsultation
  - (ii) Medical education
  - (iii) Video-Conferencing
  - (iv) Administration, etc.

(e) Tele-Consultation—For practice of Tele-cardiology, Tele-radiology, Tele-pathology, Tele-psychiatry, Tele-surgery, Tele-dermatology, etc.

4. REAL-TIME *VS.* STORE AND FORWARD ARCHITECTURE

(a) Tele-medicine transmission in Real-Time requires two or more centres exchanging information simultaneously or better known as synchronously from their respective sites and communicating inter-actively. The Real-time exchange of information can be facilitated via (i) Plain Old Telephone Services (POTS), (ii) Video-mediated transmission which includes simultaneously interview and examination of the patients, transmission of imaging of various anatomic sites, auscultation of heart and lung sounds and review of X-rays and other images (that also include pathology slides and others such as gamma camera, MRI, Ultrasound).

(b) Store and Forward Format—The S&F concept is most acceptable in clinical application. The complete patient data in the form of EPR and audio, video clip along with images are transmitted from the originator to the consultant or from one end to another via communication modalities ranging from telephone, e-mail and, more appropriately, by special and more powerful Tele-communication channels like ISDN or DSL lines. The medical information is thus compiled and stored in the format of simple ECG recording or a combination of audio, video clips and images. The digital information thus compiled is sent to the consultant or referral hospital for review interpretation and advice at his/her convenience. There is no immediate demand or compulsion on the consultant's time during his or her busy schedule. The concept can provide greater ease for advice and opinion since the information is already sent and stored in the system.

It is essential to note that each of the modalities—Real Time *vs.* Store and Forward format—has its own advantages and disadvantages, particularly in terms of their merits in clinical practice. The following Table on the next page depicts the need and utility of these concepts.

5. THE REAL-TIME INTERACTION AND TRANSMISSION

(i) Have the advantage of an immediate response to an urgent medical requirement. There is a specific need to support the primary care physician in case of emergency medicine and trauma care. It must be understood very clearly that the emergency medicine can only be served with Real-Time interaction. Store and Forward technology cannot be used for emergency and trauma situations. However, Real-Time is more time-consuming, expensive and requires enormous time of the physician and the supporting staff at both the ends of the centre.

TABLE 2

Real-Time *versus* Store and Forward

Need	Real-Time	Store & Forward
1. Interactive	Yes	No
2. Bandwidth	Requirement	Higher Lower
3. Tele-Communication costs	High	Low
4. Multimedia-transmission of data (images, sounds and video)	Yes	Yes
5. Response time	Immediate	Delayed
6. Consultant can expand on patient's history and physical findings (as in case discussion)	Yes	No
7. Instructional potential for primary health professionals (Education & continuing medical education)	Very Good	Very little
8. Convenience of use for primary physician and consultant/specialist	Poor	Very Good
9. Scheduling time and convenience	Difficult	Not necessary

(ii) The Real-Time interaction has most importantly added information and practice with the referring doctor situated at the primary or secondary health centres who can be benefited immensely by the experience of the consultants. This can prove to be a great education facility to the doctor situated in remote areas and can be used as an educational avenue to medical and health providers at the primary and secondary health care centres. The referring doctor can directly participate and can further identify the patient's problem. The consultant at the other end can request for more additional information instantaneously in the form of history of illness and even ask for more tests which have further scope for discussion in patient management. There is probably no better learning environment for primary and secondary health care personnel than that in which patients' needs are met in a setting where the physicians, at the primary and secondary end, can directly observe and participate in the patient care programme with direct and instant communication with the consulting physicians and surgeons situated in large centres and/or major teaching hospitals. The physicians at the originating site can learn and get education in this process to diagnose and treat patients more efficiently. Their vision can be broadened in clinical medicine.

(iii) The benefits notwithstanding, there are also many limitations in Real-Time interaction:

(a) It is more expensive and time-consuming than that of Store and Forward format.

(b) Teler-adiology and tele-pathology formats require and demand high resolution image acquisition and transmission lines which sometimes are not available at the primary and secondary care centres.

(c) Convenience and coordination of the schedule of consultants/specialists is not a simple proposition and has many constraints on their time and convenience.

(d) Availability of the network and provision of many more telephone lines for checking and rechecking the availability and confirming and reconfirming the arrangements is a time-consuming and expensive phenomenon.

(e) Real-Time requires high bandwidth. The current interactive audio-video standards are minimum in the range of 384 Kbps and higher speed for transmission and certainly involve high cost on telecommunication.

6. STORE AND FORWARD ARCHITECTURE

(i) The concept can be explained that the referring and consulting physician/surgeon does not have to coordinate his/her schedule within the telemedicine network and system.

(ii) There is no need for the patient to be present at the time of consultation. The referring physician and other health care providers do not have to be present as in case of Real-

Time interaction. The primary care doctor can compile and capture all the information of the patient in the form of history, patient examination, laboratory and other investigative tests and get sufficient time to complete and compile the electronic file of the patient.

(iii) The transmission of information is not highly sensitive as it can be transferred with slower speed and communication system than that of Real-Time practice. The S&F concept requires less bandwidth and also incurs minimum telecommunication cost even for transferring of large data.

(iv) The Store and Forward Technology is in fact a sophisticated e-mail where better resolution of the images, electronic patient record and other necessary information can be sent. It allows the physician to complete a package of information of a patient which is stored as a digital file and then forwarded electronically to the consultant/specialist for review, opinion and interpretation. The consultant/adviser/specialist reviews the information at his/her convenient time and communicates back to the referring physician or health-care provider. The significant advantage of S&F is that the referring and the consultant physicians/specialists do not have to coordinate their schedule with the telemedicine network programme.

(v) The referring physician and/or health care provider has sufficient time to complete all the details of the patient's history, physical examination, laboratory tests and other images pertaining to the patient performed to-date and can transmit these at a convenient time which can be even economical in transmission. This is just like a draft or composed letter from a referring physician/doctor to a specialist. This is a great benefit in the patient care programme in that adequate and complete information is collected and sent for the needful.

(vi) It is important to note that a very large digital package of clinical information of a patient or the person who needs consultation/specialist opinion can be sent over by a regular telephone line requiring no special lines like ISDN, DSL, etc., where they are not readily available. In addition, more practically, the Store and Forward system uses as low as 56 Kbps line for transmission of data. This is specially useful in primary and secondary health care system in our country where at least telephone lines are now available. The transmission will also be economical as the data can be sent at a time when the rates are cheaper.

(vii) Store and Forward technologies can play a dominant role in speciality group telemedicine programme. The most prominent among them are Tele-Radiology, Tele-Pathology and Tele-Dermatology; they constitute the greatest number of tele-consultations in the developed countries. In a country like India, the S&F concept may prove one of the very valuable facilities for consultation/opinion in the form of second or third opinion for diagnosis and management programme. In many situations, recordings like ECG can also be beneficial in Store and Forward transmission in chronic heart diseases and even in feotal monitoring for special management of pregnant mothers and in prenatal care programme.

(viii) The only disadvantage the author feel is that the S&F concept does not allow direct exchange between the consultants and the patients. The referring doctor/health care provider becomes a responsible party for collecting the necessary information of the patients for transmission to the consultant for his/her assessment and advice. In case the consultant needs additional information in the form of patient history or physical examination, this can not be provided. Also more time is required for tele-consultation. The referring physician also does not get the instant education and knowledge in the consultant's approach in finding better solutions and in the management of the patient. In other words, the educational value of Tele-consultation is considerably reduced in S&F concept which is a plus point readily available with Real-Time telemedicine practice.

7. TELEMEDICINE AND THE INTERNET

The concept of Store and Forward is fast growing due to its low cost and comparatively easy implementation. Internet perhaps seems to be particularly suitable for this kind of telemedicine application either through multimedia e-mail or web-based tools. The practice of internet presents some problems mainly the slow process of transmission and retrieval, particularly of the images. The compression techniques and software have solved this problem to some extent. However, the internet practice is still not fully utilised by the medical profession.

I. The Definition of Store and Forward

The definition of Store and Forward concept through internet can be described as a discipline where the information is recorded before or after transmission but not simultaneously. As a result, less bandwidth is required and networking do not have to be available. We must realise that this is not a new invention since radiographs and glass slides also constitute a type of "Store and Forward" concept (when sent from one place to another by post of messenger). This technique is only used when the data is acquired without any intervention from the person receiving it and using it for further study, analysis and advice. The "Store and Forward" should always be considered *vis-a-vis* Real-Time application since it is cheaper and easier to perform. However, we must realise that the user at the other end who may be a specialist, deals with sampling problems and has no complete view and data available on the patient. The technical aspect related to the technology is digital acquisition of diagnostic information. The software for compression technique to store the data, the direct communication, the use of server architecture for data delivery and the display at the expert site is an essential requirement. We must also understand the different types of Store and Forward formats such as audio transfer, data and text transmission and still or moving images, using the examples of heart sounds, Tele-ECG, Tele-Radiology and ultrasound video images. In Tele-Dermatology, Tele-Radiology, Tele-

Pathology and Tele-Cardiology, the multimedia e-mail is used through highly technical format specially to offer the security for the confidentiality. In one of the presentations in Heidelberg (Germany) during a meeting in September 1999, Dr. Dell Mea said, in his concluding remarks, that Store and Forward through internet, sometimes, was the only way to offer remote medical services. This is because of the lack of infrastructure, different time zones between countries and large data transmission. He further emphasised that we must identify the need when this technique (internet transmission) can be used in clinical practice. Dr. Klaus Worle from the University of Rosenburg (Germany) highlighted during his presentation the use of standard internet technology and wavelet compression to limit and considerably reduce the download time of the images taken at the hospitals where the consultation is needed. Another speaker Dr. Jack Woodall (Netherland) gave his impression and illustration with Store and Forward concept that e-mail can solve communication problem for the third world countries in health care programme. He further informed that the requirements of ground stations can be a very useful tool for e-mail services. The station can be even switched down for a limited period of 6-8 hours a day to save expenses. Dr. Joe Hovel from Australia discussed, during the same meeting, on Telemedicine practice, using the Internet that health professionals in Australia have started using e-mail, the mobile telephone and desk-top computers for communication with colleagues, patients and clients. He described that internet medicine covers a vast remote country side in Australian rural health centres with minimum input and infrastructure. Prof. Kontaxakis from Germany discussed the development of portable 3-D ultrasound telemedicine network workstation for use in isolated regions, areas of calamity, and in some of the developing countries. The system which he described as "Tele-in-vivo" includes a personal computer, ultrasound equipment, the in-vivo software for free hand scanning in 3-D, a modem, ISDN lines, Ethernet and collaboration facilities. The basic infrastructure is not an expensive proposition in Store and forward tele-medicine practice through the Internet.

The Internet practice in health care is one of the practical alternatives to dynamic telemedicine system where the hardware are expensive. The practice requires high band-width and trained medical and technical personnel. There are several web sites developed and introduced for internet-based physician consultation system. One of the sites known as Medical-Electronically Link (MEL) was established at Dartmouth Hitchcock Medical Centre in New Hampshire (USA) by using the World Wide Web. The benefits of MEL are:

(a) Low cost hardware and bandwidth channel,

(b) Accessibility,

(c) Self-explanatory interface,

(d) Convenience, and

(e) Its use as Store and Forward format.

The system is also implemented at the family practice clinics in Manchester (NH, USA) and at the Tribhuvan University Teaching Hospital, Kathmandu, Nepal. This is the most practical and cost-effective system in telemedicine technology. In clinical practice, if a physician needs input and consultation of a specialist, he can have access to World Wide Web and Internet into a department-specific consultation practice. The requesting physician can also include digitized images of anything related to the case such as physical examination findings, page(s) from the patient chart, an ECG or an X-ray film. All this information is stored, chronological order on patient's records for further advice and consultation. If there is an update required of the progress of the patient, this can also be sent in the same file as an attachment. The advice can be stored in the system and can be retrieved by the referring physician.

There is a growing interest for low-cost telemedicine tools in all areas, especially Tele-Radiology, the Tele-Pathology and Tele-Dermatology. The main interest in the application is the usual telemedicine application, i.e. tele-diagnosis, distant learning and teaching, remote imaging and data processing and quality control. However, tele-diagnosis is the most important and prominent application and in case of pathology and radiology, it could evolve two distinct diagnostic workup:

- ❑ Remote Expert Consultation, and
- ❑ Intra-operative frozen section service for instant pathology report.

The main area of interest is the second or third opinion from an expert(s) to the requesting physician and surgeon when a difficult case is encountered during their practice.

2. Diagnosis and Consultation in Pathology

Anatomic pathology aims at morphologically studying lesions induced by the disease and in turn at providing useful information for obtaining correct diagnosis and to establish prompt treatment and progress. Pathology is an image-based discipline where a diagnosis is achieved by examining perceivable features from images obtained in many ways; first of all from light microscope images thus representing the main sources of knowledge and information. In routine pathologist's glance the success lies through the microscopic findings at different magnifications, and looking for diagnostic features. When something is found related to the available clinical details to identify from one or more possible diagnoses this forms the opinion. Sometimes the complexity of the case makes it necessary to request for the so-called second opinion and advice from other specialists, possibly an expert in the specific field who has more experience and expertise.

We can distinguish two levels of consultation which is necessary for the diagnosis:

- ❑ Between the colleagues of the same department and the institute; and
- ❑ External consultants and experts in the specific field of the disease and the organ.

We must know that both levels of second opinion consultation are very important issues in pathology. The latter (external consultation) involves the communication channel with an expert located either within country or elsewhere in the world.

3. Consultation through Store and Forward in Tele-Pathology

The basic idea of introducing Store and Forward format in Tele-pathology is to select and acquire diagnostically representative images from glass-slides and to send them to the remote consultants by means of some telematic channel. The complete preparation of a case thus includes image selection and acquisition, store in appropriate format, aggregation with clinical data and finally transmission to distant sites.

(i) Image Acquisition

There are two systems of acquiring images from microscope:

- ❑ by means of analog techniques, and
- ❑ by means of digital camera.

The former needs also a frame grabber card into the computer, which converges the analog signal coming from the camera into digital values. The usually available devices are based on:

- ❑ a single input chip (Mono CCD), and
- ❑ three separated chips for red, green and blue colour component (3 CCD).

These are preferably for pathology images due to their higher quality. The resolution is up to 600 lines and with colour resolution of 24 bits. The images are acquired up to 30 frames per second. The digital devices have a digital output and are connected through a computer by direct connection to the SCSI "bus" or other high-speed connection. The digital cameras and photo scanners reach a higher spatial and colour resolution up to 5000 x 5000 pixels. This is mainly adequate for Store and Forward tele-pathology technology.

The still images acquisition allows higher resolution than that of dynamic Real Time technology because the need for Real Time does not make it possible to adopt very high resolution images since this occupies a large amount of memory. The optical resolution of microscopic images depends on the objective magnification and the higher magnification starts from 20X. The resolution obtained with CCD cameras is adequate for capturing all the information from the 20X magnification, while at low magnification, greater resolution is needed to reach the same quality of images. In routine practice we can use very high-resolution devices for acquiring low magnification images from the whole biopsy material and hence it is not necessary for the selection of field.

4. Storage and Compression Issues

In usual practice an image of 640 x 480 pixels and 24 bit colour needs 900 Kbps of Storage space. In the image for 2000 x 3000 pixels, which is a typical size of a high-end digital camera, the Storage value goes up to 13.6 Megabytes. The transmission time, we know, depends on the image file size and the bytes value. We need to apply the technology and use the compression algorithms in order to reduce the file size of the image. The compression techniques can be described and classified into the following:

(a) Loss less, i.e., completely reversible, and
(b) Loss—with some loss of information when compressed and decompressed.

The former (Loss less) technique allows for compression ratio only up to 3:1. The latter (Lossy) is better technology where the compression ratio is in the range of 100-200 : 1 and is known to be more efficient. The most common Lossy technique is JPEG (Joint Photographic Expert Group) developed to exploit eye and camera limitations for discharging unuseful information from images. In Store and Forward technology JPEG has been widely applied in compression ratio up to 30 : 1 in practice.

There is also another way of compression of Storage and file size. This is the colour reduction from 24 to 8 bits which means that the number of available different colours decreased from millions to only 256 and the file size becomes one-third of the original one. Further, on such files a loss less compression can be further applied by colour reduction technology. However, we must understand that the colour should be reduced by specific adoptive algorithm for diagnostic equivalence.

5. File Formats

There is an essential requirement of using some standard for effective interchanges of images when they are stored. Currently, the TIFF/format is being used for 8 bits, loss less compressed images. Further, TIFF is adequate for 24 bits loss less compressed images and the JIFI (usually called JPEG) hosts JPEG compressed images. We must also know that still there is no real standardisation available for the whole case, i.e., aggregation of clinical data and images. The current implementation uses proprietary formats, or HTML or STML as a document framework but with some limitation due to currently poor cementing structurisation. In future, the formats will be overtaken by XML standard.

6. Delivery of Cases

Once the images have been acquired and aggregated into clinical data, the transmission can be undertaken. A correct implementation should utilise all the steps making reliable Store and Forward communication, i.e., by dealing with errors and abnormal situations and considering the security and privacy of the data. The Internet e-mail which has been used in different trials and projects as a means for Store and Forward, Tele-pathology and Tele-radiology can be considered adequate in this application. We must accept that it is a correct approach in clinical practice and we should see the underutilising modern system in transmission of our clinical material for discussion, opinion and advice.

8. APPLICATION IN CLINICAL PRACTICE

Telemedicine is one of the disciplines in Information Technology and is one of the media in clinical practice of Medicine and Medical Education. In the developed countries, Telemedicine is a reality and culturally accepted. The health facility is even entering into home-care health delivery services as well. Telemedicine is a new technology where powerful telecommunication channels and computers are used in transmission of medical information in the form of images, patient data and record, voice of the patients and of the specialist over short and long distances. In recent years, the spread of computer communication network, the substantial reduction in the cost of equipment and the introduction of Real Time audio-video transmission technology have added a new dimension to Telemedicine application in clinical practice.

In India, Telemedicine can be put to use for utilisation of the vast resources of our medical specialists and super specialists available in the metropolitan and large cities and some of the institutions of national and international standing. Our patients can be immensely benefited by the experience of our professionals, more so of specially specialists and super-specialist, in effecting improvement in patient care and their management by facilitating prompt diagnosis and treatment. The Primary and Community health care centres whose working is still far from satisfactory can be improved with Telemedicine application when we can provide consultation, opinion and advice to the patients. In addition, the Continuing Medical Education to the physicians who are otherwise professionally isolated in these centres, particularly these located in remote areas, becomes a continuing process in its real sense. They have no direct or indirect links with their counterparts in major hospitals situated even in the region, let alone those situated in the State and Country. The impact of this development will be immediately visible at the primary and secondary centres (who bear the brunt of providing health care to the rural community) where a large number of professionals and specialists can be "inducted" to enhance the quality and quantity in our existing network. It is now becoming possible that with the growing telemedicine application, more and more people can be benefited by the services of specialists and super specialists. It is hoped that when the patients, physicians and the consultants can meet and interact electronically, many barriers to accessing care will certainly provide a more comprehensive service to the patients in remote areas and semi-urban areas as well. We must realise that consultation with specialists through telemedicine technology can achieve the diagnosis more quickly and a definite treatment plan can be implemented without losing precious time. More importantly, utilisation of local and regional services can be facilitated more appropriately and convincingly for patient care through telemedicine application. Telemedicine has the potential for a greater positive effect on the future of health care than any other modalities and it can bring high quality care to our people, especially those who are presently deprived of even the basic medical care in rural, semi-urban and remote areas. In additional, it can provide a lifeline to medical expertise when and wherever it is needed.

4 CHAPTER

Challenges in Telemedicine

INTRODUCTION

The recent developments in the field of communication and computer technology have completely revolutionised the method in which the individuals and business can enter. The new technology in the practice of medicine has also taken a new direction in the developments where the physicians, surgeons and other health workers can extend their support in patient care programme. The most important area of interest is the primary and secondary health care where a large number of specialists can be inducted in the health care delivery. It is now becoming possible with the growing telemedicine application that more and more people can be benefited by the services of specialists and super-specialists. When the patient and the physician can meet and interact electronically, many barriers to accessing care will disappear gradually. There is no doubt that some of the medical activities will certainly require direct physical contact between the patient and the doctor. The future technology may overcome this situation and the specialist can virtually put hand on the patient. Many interactions can be conducted without the patient and/or the doctor having to travel between one place to another. The travel time will be completely eliminated and the waiting time of the doctor will also be considerably reduced.

The enhanced efficiency through the practice of telemedicine will provide more comprehensive services to the patient. Consultation with specialists through telemedicine technology can achieve a definite diagnosis more quickly and certainly a comprehensive treatment plan can be implemented without losing time. In addition, many follow-up visits can be accomplished with telemedicine and many more follow-up visits can be undertaken in the interest of the patient and his/her treatment. It is important that the patients in rural areas can be benefited tremendously and also that the patients can get more time and access to the most appropriate level of care. Early medical intervention can reduce the morbidity and mortality. The convenience factor for the patient has the greatest advantage in Telemedicine practice in that the travel and transportation from rural to urban centres is considerably reduced. The patient in a rural setting has to spend a significant amount of time on travel through busy traffic to a centre or a doctor or a specialist located in major towns. More importantly, utilisation of local and regional resources can be facilitated through telemedicine. These rural/semi-urban centres can be improved with the direct contact of specialists/consultants and many tests that could be performed in rural and semi-urban centres can be performed with the support and demand of the consultants. In other words, these centres (rural and semi-urban) will improve gradually and function better and expand their scope in patient care programme. Further, when the tests' results and images are shared with the specialists through telemedicine technology, there is every likelihood that the tests will not be duplicated as is the practice in most of the cities at present. The practice of telemedicine will allow the primary and secondary physicians to remain more involved in the patient care when they are in direct touch and contact with the specialists or higher level consultants in the region. This essentially results in better community care. The physicians/surgeons who communicate at higher level certainly establish closer working relationship.

They become more familiar with each other and greater confidence is gained and ultimately the patient is the beneficiary.

TELEMEDICINE TECHNOLOGY

Telemedicine Practice involves the use of computers and telecommunication equipment to provide health care over long distances. It is actually an expansion of one of the oldest, simplest and most popular forms of medical consultation—a telephone conversation between a doctor and his patient or a general medical practitioner and a specialist. But, unlike the telephone, telemedicine technology uses interactive conferencing—a Real Time consultation and transmission of patient data in the form of audio, video, texts and images.

1. Real Time Video Conferencing

Real Time Video Conferencing also known as interactive tele-conferencing using existing telephone lines or preferably ISDN lines for better results and faster transmission of patient data. The technique permits a doctor and his patient to confer simultaneously even though they are located at different sites. The establishment is simple, not expensive, where a video camera in an examination room would enable the primary care or secondary care doctor to present the patient to another doctor, a specialist or a consultant at the other end. The doctor at the other end usually is a consultant and would also be in front of the camera and will offer his/her opinion. The same technology is also used for educational purposes where the medical students in remote locations attend the lectures delivered by consultants and eminent scientists in their respective specialisations. In addition, doctors, nurses and other health professionals are also benefited by the continuing medical education programme which is an essential ingredient in updating them on newer developments in Medicine.

2. Transmission of Medical Images

This technology involves creating and transmitting of

medical images such as X-rays and histopathology slides electronically in the form digital signals from one location to another. The expert at a distant site receives the images, evaluates them, helps in making a diagnosis and supports in additional care as and when needed. This process is much like sending an X-ray by mail or courier service but with Telemedicine the transmission is almost instantaneous. The technology can also support in compressing the digitised images further and thereby reducing transmission time and storage requirements. This results in quality, when it is viewed as a restructured image is generally not reduced using the recent development in technology programme.

In Summary, Telemedicine Technology can make a radical difference in health care delivery in rural and semi-urban communities where, generally, access to specialised care is often sporadic (practically not available) and patients and their relatives may hesitate to travel long distances to see a doctor. With Telemedicine, the patient can benefit from the expertise of a distant specialist and can seek treatment at the community level hospitals. In one of the studies from Georgia (USA) Telemedicine Network, it was reported that the practice of telemedicine has been able to demonstrate that almost 80 per cent of the patients seen by the specialists through telemedicine never left their hometowns. They also found that Telemedicine was cost-effective and most convenient to the primary care doctors. They further reported that Telemedicine was also used to provide services to prisoners who otherwise would have to be moved with great caution and at additional cost because of the need for guards to accompany the prisoners during their transportation. The report further reveals that a mobile telemedicine van comes to the prison on a regular basis, plugs in and allows the health care professionals to conduct medical check-ups of the inmates at site.

3. Home-Care

Telemedicine Technology would be used for home-based follow-up of critically ill-patients, elderly persons located at a distance and would help monitor the patients of diabetes or asthma or similar illnesses at home, thus avoiding hospitalisation unless it is truly necessary. Similarly, high-risk patients with heart problems would have their ECG and blood pressure readings monitored in home environment by telemetry programme. The computerised service can facilitate this type of care which has been developed to monitor various health signs. This service helps the patients to check their blood pressure and undergo ECG at home and send the results via modem to the health care providers. In some of the centres in the USA and Europe, home-care services are now under clinical trial where its use can cut down hospital stay and emergency visits by the patients who are recovering in home environment.

4. Limitations

There are some obstacles and apprehensions in the use of Telemedicine technology in the rural and semi-urban centres as well as in home care delivery. The medical liability is the real issue especially a remote specialist who cannot put his or her hand on examination and this could be regarded as delivery of less than adequate patient care. Further, a compressed digital image may not be reconstructed well and, hence, valuable information may be lost. In this situation, a doctor could possibly face a malpractice suit (especially in developed countries). These technical problems notwithstanding, experts advise, the patients to give Telemedicine a trial. In one of the reports Dr. Brick (from West Virginia Telemedicine programme) said: "Go into it with an open mind". He further said, "Expect to be able to see and hear the doctor from the other end. Expect the doctors to connect with you and personalise the experience for you. Talk to him. Ask whatever questions you have just as you would have in an end-person consultation." It is only a matter of time, we hope, before these obstacles are overcome and doctors and public become more aware of telemedicine practice. It is said that if 20 years ago, someone had said, you could walk up to a machine, press a few buttons, and get the cash (from an automatic teller machine—ATM), you would have said it is incredible. But, like automatic teller machine, one of the pioneer and initial users said, the professionals and patients eventually will accept telemedicine.

5. Telecommunication Network

Telecommunication Network is a major area in clinical practice of telemedicine. The communication services still have major problems in any developing country, including India. No doubt, there is a rapid pace of development and there has been consistent improvement in the telecommunication services and their deployment. Fast transmission of data is still far from satisfactory and needs definite improvement. A telephone having 28-56 Kbps is not capable of data transmission, especially images and graphics. ISDN lines are still not available in many cities and, even where they are available, they are not yet customaries for the use of Telemedicine technology. The staff in telecommunication is still untrained in the ISDN lines. The rates of the services, especially ISDN, are also expensive. The rates must come down. A large bandwidth is essentially needed to carry a video or other signals between sophisticated and user equipment which may also prove prohibitive for a modest rural clinic located at a distance from the desired connection. The planners and the users in Telemedicine technology must come closer and support the practice of tele-communication technology with adequate bandwidth and digital lines.

6. Registration with State Medical Council

Physicians and other health-care practitioners are required to obtain license from the State in which they practice or from the Central Medical Council. In a country like the USA, it is necessary to obtain from respective State. However, in India the medical practitioners and specialists are permitted to practice in any State though the registration may have been done with some other State. In a recent publication of the American College of Radiology, they have given a direction that all the physicians who provide the official and authenticated interpretation of images transmitted by tele-radiology should obtain full and unrestricted license from that State where the patient is located. This is to avoid unnecessary litigation and future developments in malpractice suits. The Federation of the State Medical Boards has advised that the law would require a special medical license for physicians practising across state boundaries. They further stated that an expedition review procedure for obtaining the special telemedicine license should be implemented at the earliest. Similar to the grant of licenses there are credentialing references to the requirement imposed by individual health care facilities on practitioners. Many hospitals would require a physician to undergo the credentialing process in order to treat patients at their hospitals. These issues, however, are not applicable in our own context in India. Even though medical and health services is a State subject, doctors are permitted to practice and continue to be able to practise anywhere in India with registration in any State/Union Territory. The situation may require some kind of standard governance in telemedicine practice in India as well. We must see the enhanced benefits in the services and ensure access to high quality care, while reducing waiting time and transport cost especially for rural and semi-urban patients. There are definite benefits to be derived from Telemedicine services.

7. Confidentiality of Patients

Identifiable Medical Information

The need of protecting the confidentiality of electronic patient records is an essential requirement and this is under discussion for many years now to find a model for confidentiality of the record. This is particularly important since the medical practice requires transmission of patient record to other centres and consultants for advice and opinion. In a country like the USA, there is a system that every state has different laws and different levels of protection of this information. However, in our country although Health is a concurrent subject, yet the patient can go from one State to another for advice, opinion and treatment. The main concern, I feel, is the use of medical record for publication and research which may pose difficult problems in a country like India in the sense that they can publish the information without consent of the institution, hospital or the patient. We must understand that it is difficult to effectively enforce restrictions when the information is transferred from one place to another. Therefore, suitable solutions may be worked out in Telemedicine practice. We must not forget that when access to computerised medical information has to become easier the commercial value of the computerised information and medical data-base may have increased substantially and, in addition make these records more vulnerable to misuse, abuse and disclosure. We must workout a solution that confidential information will receive more reliable form of protection.

8. Medical Malpractice Liability

There is a lack of clarity on the question whether the physicians are protected by their insurance companies when practising telemedicine. This is a significant factor relevant to the growth of telemedicine application. Some of the issues need understanding and answers. These can be described as follows:

(i) Whether a physician-patient relation is created.

(ii) Standards of telemedical care, especially the equipment used and transmission rates and bandwidth of the telecommunication link between the patient and the doctor and between one centre and another.

(iii) Whether informed consent of the patient is to be taken for telemedicine advice and opinion.

This is more applicable in the USA and European countries. However, we may come across a real case in India for which we must prepare ourselves and formulate some kind of legislation in concurrence with Medical Council of India and the State Medical authority.

5

CHAPTER

Telemedicine—Its Needs and Benefits

The Telemedicine system can improve rural health care especially primary and secondary care of patients attending community and district hospitals. The technology can improve professional interaction between rural health professionals and their colleagues with urban medical specialists. We must understand that the quality of interaction between distant physicians becomes significantly improved when they communicate via telemedicine networks because it conveys more than just their voices through telephone conversation and discussion. The Store and Forward architecture in Telemedicine system allows consultants and specialists to share images, sound clips and graphical data of the patients, not confined to verbal discussion. The interactive and synchronous video conferencing allows physicians and distant specialists to interact with each other along with their patients and not just voices on telephone. We must realise that in Telemedicine technology the whole nature of interaction between the physicians along with the information (patient's record) conveyed to them is greatly enhanced. In fact, this is a face-to-face discussion for advice and opinion between the patients and their physicians located at different and distant places.

Telemedicine can also provide high quality educational opportunities to rural and semi-urban medical professionals from specialists and super-specialists located in urban areas. Both audio and video conferencing networks are used to provide educational opportunities to physicians and other health workers in their communities without having to leave their practice and location. The practice of Telemedicine allows them to attend more "conferences" (virtual classrooms) and exposure to newer knowledge and latest developments. Telemedicine Technology exposes rural and semi-urban physicians to newer medical technologies as used in urban environment. With the Store and Forward concept, the rural physicians and surgeons can have instant access to medical data and they can involve themselves in the study and use of modern diagnostic tools and imaging devices. With video telemedicine system, the rural physicians and surgeons can literally observe medical procedures being conducted on their patients and virtually keep themselves involved in greater patient care.

Telemedicine System has promise to solidify the referral relationship and the physicians and surgeons can communicate at higher levels, establish working relations, become more familiar with each other's capabilities and expertise and, in addition, they tend to share patient information more consistently. This supports a very close working relationship with urban specialists and super-specialists. Telemedicine practice may be helpful in sustaining and keeping the health professionals in rural areas. **This can indeed be a blessing to the administration in providing a balanced health delivery system. When the patient along with the primary and secondary care physicians 'visits' the specialists via telemedicine system, the expert advice and opinion are readily available. The physician is both directly and indirectly involved on behalf of the patient.**

The penetration of Telemedicine into rural areas places the rural doctor at par with his urban/semi-urban counterpart so far as availability of modern facilities and expert advice is concerned. **In a country like India, where almost 80 per cent**

of its population lives in rural areas and where the doctors usually shy away from serving in rural areas, the introduction of Telemedicine will prove a single significant factor in ensuring social justice in our health care delivery. This will certainly improve quality health care at the grassroots level.

More and more services can be provided to patients locally under the guidance of expert advice and opinion provided by a distant specialist via Telecommunication. In addition, Telemedicine provides and facilitates more and more follow-up of the patients in rural community. The specialist can instruct the local physician on the advice to be given to the patient during follow-up visits which he/she (the local doctor) is otherwise unfamiliar. The scope of improvement in patient care by the local physician is thus expanded and at the same time the patient does not need to travel and can avoid inconvenience in terms of both physical discomfort and transport cost.

In one of the published reports, the rural physicians have admitted that their decision to accept rural assignments was positively influenced by the fact that the community hospitals were a part of the Telemedicine network programme. They further informed that they were satisfied with their work and clinical practice. The report reveals that the 'specialist' cover provided by the telemedicine network was really a distinct advantage.

CONSULTANT, SPECIALIST AND SUPER-SPECIALIST IN THE MAJOR CITIES AND URBAN AREAS

The specialists and super-specialists working in referral centres that support the rural and semi-urban medical services can also be benefited from Telemedicine programme. This can be described as follows:

(1) The specialists can often do much of the spadework of a difficult case remotely (the local site) and can save their precious time. The work is

done by the primary and secondary care physicians can narrow down the differential diagnosis of a difficult case.

(2) This also helps in proper and further consultation for management. The patient can directly go to the right specialist right at the first time thereby saving the precious time both the patient and the health delivery system.

BENEFITS TO THE PATIENTS

The rural and semi-urban patients are the greatest beneficiaries of telemedicine technology. Patients can get more timely access to the most appropriate level of care and early intervention results in reducing the morbidity and mortality. There will be a significant reduction in transportation cost of the patients who participate and take advantage of Tele-consultation over the networking programme. The convenience factor (both for the patients and the doctors), which is perhaps not given due consideration, is the most important component in telemedicine technology practice. In one of the studies reported, as early as from Eastern Montana (USA), Telemedicine network demonstrated that more than 50 per cent of the patients were satisfied with tele-consultation programme and they could talk in person with the specialists and super-specialists situated far away. Almost hundred percent patients admitted that they would prefer to use telemedicine system instead of visiting the city clinics and specialist hospitals. The patients were able to feel the positive impact of telemedicine in their care and health delivery programme.

OVERALL BENEFITS

It has been proved in some of the studies that Telemedicine Technology has facilitated the utilisation of the local/regional resources to the maximum. The results of the laboratory tests, images and patient data transmitted to the specialists via telemedicine can be further used and there will be no repetition and duplication of the tests when the patients visit the specialists in the city hospitals for further investigation and treatment. Telemedicine practice allows the primary care physicians to be in constant touch with and to take care of their patients during reference and consultation with the specialist. This reference, in fact, results in better continuity in care and close association between the doctor and the patient.

In addition, Telemedicine can prove most beneficial to the entire health care system in the region and permit more rapid success to the most appropriate level of medical services. This system will prove most economical and cost-effective in developing countries where specialist and super-specialist services are not readily available and are also an expensive proposition.

THE NEED FOR TELEMEDICINE IN URBAN HEALTH CARE PROGRAMME

The Telemedicine network in urban and metropolitan cities can be used on the same pattern as that of primary and secondary health care programme.

It is a common feature with physicians in urban and metropolitan areas to practise at multiple hospitals, in addition to their own practice at their site and premises. The urban residents may also have to travel to a significant distance to have access to specialist-physician's care. There are invariably longer waiting time and getting an early appointment is difficult. This certainly delays the process of seeking the advice and opinion of the specialist. It is also seen that in urban settings patients usually take consultation and advice from multiple specialists for the same or different conditions and ailments. This approach on the part of the patient can complicate their diagnosis and treatment.

We should also realise that when a patient is seen by more than one physician/specialist, each and every physician and consultant has to maintain a separate record in his/her clinic and hospital. Moreover, this very record is not readily available to the other specialists when they need it. It is extremely important that in order to provide a definitive care and treatment to the patient, there must be some kind of interaction or exchange of opinion between the physicians/ specialists whom the patient is consulting for further management. Some mechanism should be devised to ensure availability of the records of the patients to the other physicians as well. The complexity of the physician-patient relationship and the subsequent consultation with other physicians and specialists demand establishment of an information management system in urban facilities and settings. Telemedicine with medical informatics can definitely meet the demand for efficient maintenance of the records of patients electronically, including imaging and data. The efficiency of the specialist/consultant with the help of computerised patient record can be improved and duplication of investigations may be minimised. The physician should be able to have access to all the necessary patient data/ information, studies and test results whenever and wherever they are needed. Telemedicine will decrease the need for physician's travel between the specialities and sub-specialities. He may be benefited particularly in having information sent to him (specialist) well in advance before visiting because the video telemedicine system will bring the patients to the physician without transportation. The sub-specialist physician can consult on a patient without having to be in the surgical operation theatre and hospital premises. Tele-Radiology systems allow Radiologists to see and study films from multiple establishments, especially as and when the examinations are being conducted sitting in their own office and clinic.

THE SPECIALIST-RESOURCES UTILISATION

The inadequate and limited availability of specialists and sub-specialists with the health care delivery system can be met with the Telemedicine Technology Network. Centralisation of specialists within a health care organisation is also possible. Specialists like Pathologists, Radiologists, Dermatologists and Psychiatrists can provide consultation to multiple facilities within a health care system without losing productivity as a result of reducing their travel from one place to another. The specialists whose ability to reach broad target population was limited by time and travel constraints will now be available to more patients. Telemedicine will further reduce the delay in getting specialist's opinion due to transportation time and/or on account of non-availability of record and data of the patient.

ACCESS TO CARE

The patient and the physician can meet and interact electronically. Many barriers and obstacles to extending care will disappear. We must not forget that some medical activities will always require direct physical contact between the patient and the physician. We should take the advantage of accessibility through Telemedicine Technology.

Many organisations are exploring the possibilities of "Care Contract" for their employees at their workplace and access to telemedicine services. When the health care services can be provided at the workplace and early intervention can result in decreased morbidity. Telemedicine practice can reduce the leave and off-time taken by the employees.

In summary, Telemedicine can provide more comprehensive services to every citizen bringing information and physician resources together for better care and improved health delivery system. A definite diagnosis can be achieved more quickly; a definite treatment plan can be implemented without losing time with tele-medicine consultation by making use of specialist/consultant's expertise and experience. Telemedicine further helps in improving the access of patients to the physician and also to make follow up visits more frequent and effective.

6

CHAPTER

Components of Telemedicine Technology and Infrastructure

The components and infrastructure in Telemedicine system consist of equipment and procedures to acquire and present clinical information and to store and retrieve data of the patient. The acquisition and presentation through Telemedicine technologies include tele-conferencing, data digitizing and display (such as, X-ray, laboratory tests), and image processors such as, video cameras and monitors. The data, storage and retrieval include storage devices (hard disc and CD ROM) along with software technology to compress, transmit and store the data at the other end. It should be understood right at the initial stage that each site should have the basic equipment for communicating with other site(s) in its network and telemedicine application. The requirement of services is the same irrespective of whether they need to be provided within a clinic, between clinics and general practitioners or in a wide area network for consultation with specialists and super-specialists.

The following are considered essential components of Telemedicine application and technology.

1. Telecommunication Infrastructure,
2. Telemedicine Infrastructure, and
3. Telemedicine Application.

The first two components are the systems that can be applied to any area of Information Technology and its application.

I. TELECOMMUNICATION INFRASTRUCTURE AND NETWORKING

This is the technology to move the information electronically from one site to another and to the geographically dispersed locations. The technology links the participating institutions, clinics and centres by electronic networking.

2. TELEMEDICINE INFRASTRUCTURE

Consists of equipment and procedures used to acquire the physical and clinical information and store the data in the computer for further analysis, study and retrieval. The acquisition and presentation technology consists of the following:

(a) Tele-conferencing,

(b) Data digitizing and display (e.g. remote X-ray, laboratory tests),

(c) Texts Processors (e.g. scanning and fax), and

(d) Image Processors (e.g. video camera and monitors).

The data storage and retrieval require: (a) Storage devices in the form of hard disc, tape and compact disc (CD), and (b) technology to compress for storage and transmission. It must be noted that most of these technologies have more general application. However, some are unique to telemedicine specially the physical and clinical information of the patients and their laboratory tests including images.

3. TELEMEDICINE APPLICATIONS

Telemedicine Applications are the health care delivery between two or more locations. The application can be classified into four categories for better understanding:

(a) Remote interactive communication between the patient and the physician and physician to physician. (Real Time Telemedicine practice).

(b) Non-interactive transmission and storage of clinical data and images for interpretation (Store and Forward concept).

(c) Medical Education—Continuing Medical Education to professionals and paramedical personnel.

(d) Medical Administration—Consultation with the District and State headquarters for instant and speedy decision-making and advice from authorities.

1. Telecommunication Infrastructures and Networking

The largest and the most accessible network is the Public Switch Network, which is operated mainly by telephone companies (in India by the Department of Telecommunication DOT). They maintain the local as well as long distance calls. The Public Network is a common carrier and is available to anyone or any organisation for its use and application. Most of the telemedical services using the public network are traditional voice and data transmission as a requirement. Ideally, we should have a public network on which we can easily make data of video call as we are now doing with a simple phone transmission as in case of telephone. It should also greatly facilitate, ease and expanse of availability to information service, e.g., a patient in a rural clinical could "visit" a specialist at a distance via a high definition video link which is sufficient for showing electronic patient record data and images particularly of X-rays and other images in sufficient quality in the patient-physician exchange programme. The following are the factors on which telecommunication technology can be discussed:

(i) Bandwidth Requirements

This can simply be defined as a frequency or spectrum measured in cycles per second between two or more transmission channels. This is termed Hertz per second (Hz). This is a measure of information carrying capacity of a communication channel. The range of frequency is directly proportional to the transmission of data with minimum loss. The transmission of information in telemedicine technology is the mixture of audio, video, data and images of the patient in the form of Electronic Patient Record (EPR). The carrying capacity of the channel, which in common language is known as "Pipe", has a direct relationship with the functions of the speed at which the information travels (transmission time) and the quality of images and data received and displayed at the receiving end. The higher the carrying capacity, the faster is the transmission of information with better quality at the receiving end. It is a well-known fact that the speed and the amount of transmission into a telecommunication channel are directly proportional to the cost and should be kept in view in case the budget is limited.

The unit of measurement of the bandwidth is kilobytes per second (Kbps). This is, in fact, a unit of measurement for the digital lines and in normal course does not apply to a regular analog telephone line. The telephone lines are better known as Plain Old Telephone Service (POTS). The range of digital lines are 56 or 64 Kbps. The difference between 56 and 64 Kbps only relates to the method in which the digital signal is transmitted and controlled from one end to the other. The telecommunication service provides us the use of one or the other method or even both in their system. A single Kbps line is generally called DSO (DSO). In telecommunication practice, the individual DSO is combined to provide a large bandwidth. The most common bandwidths used in Telemedicine practice are in the range of 128 and 384 Kbps. Recently, 1.5 Mbps (Mega bits per second) is also available. The latter (Mega bits) is also known as T-1 Telecommunication channel. The following Table shows the bandwidth terminology described above.

TABLE 3

Bandwidth	*Common Terminology in Practice*	*Increments of*
64 Kbps	DS—O	1
128 Kbps	—	2
384 Kbps	1/4T-1	6
768 Kbps	½ T-1	12
1544 Kbps (1.5 Mbps)	T-1/DS-1	24
45 Mbps	DS-3	672

(ii) Intra-facility Network

This is a network facility for electronic data transmission from the point of acquisition to the other point or many more points in the same compound or institution's buildings and/or offices. In a hospital setting or a clinic, the point of acquisition and the end point is located in the centre or a special site in a building or a hospital where doctors, nurses and technicians can work independently or under a joint programme. This can be called a centralised facility. This facility needs to be in a central location for convenience and better utilisation. The intra-facilities network can be classified into two broad categories:

(a) Simple System, and

(b) Complex System or Higher Facility.

(a) In the *simple system,* the technology is practised between two points only for transmission and consultation. The requirement is only one single cable from one point to the other.

(b) *The Complex network category system*: This system consists of a high bandwidth optic fibre with co-axial cable distribution with multiple bridges, routers and switches. Here many more points are installed with individual desk-top computers where everyone has access to the data including transmission of audio, video clips and images. The system is commonly known as Local Area Network (LAN). It should be known that LAN has high bandwidth capabilities and it works only over a relatively limited and short distance, particularly in a campus of an institution, an educational centre or a hospital.

(iii) *Inter-facility Network*: This carries the audio, video clip and data (including text and images) between two or more distant sites. These networks consist of a telecommunication line provided by the department of telecommunication services of the country. The telecommunication lines that connect the distant points are commonly known as Wide Area Network (WAN). There are two types of long distance networking facilities as:

(a) Dedicated Networking Lines, and

(b) Switch Networking Lines.

(a) *The Dedicated Network*: Consists of those communication lines that connect one or more sites on a full-time basis and in commercial terms known as Leased Lines. They are available in all the bandwidth ranging from 56 Kbps to 4-5 Mbps (However, in India these are available only up to 1.5 Mbps.) These are fixed bandwidth circuit provided by the government undertakings or private carriers for the sole and exclusive use of a customer or a hospital.

(b) *Switch Networking Lines*: These are similar to those of telephone exchange system where each user has a "unique" address in the form of a telephone number. When the party or the user calls for connection, the signal from the calling party is routed through a series of switches (in the telephone exchange) so as to reach the destination, i.e., the other party or a point. This is also called "on-dial-up-services." These special lines can operate at flexible bandwidth or a call by call basis. There are three kinds of lines available with single, two or three Bri. The cost is based on the bandwidth (64, 128 or 384

Kbps) used for Telecommunication. The cost of the call also depends upon the distance between point-to-point and time used for transmission. In a dedicated or leased line, a fixed amount is paid on an yearly basis irrespective of the use. However, the cost depends upon the bandwidth and, of course, the distance between the point to point of the lines connected.

LOCAL AREA NETWORK (LAN)

A. Configuration and Factors

B. The Store and Forward Architecture

C. Network Termination Equipment

A. Configuration and Factors

(i) Distance from the End-user Equipment to the Demarcation Point

In the case of home-care telemedicine the distance from the end-user equipment in the patient's home to the consultation room may be only a small distance and this requires simple standard telephone line.

In case of a large medical complex where the distance is many times more than the home-care, this requires a complete complex computer network to get transmission of information from point to point.

(ii) Number of Points of Acquisition and/or Display

In case of single location there is nothing more than a single wire for transmission from one point to another. This is the most simple technology. In a higher telemedicine network where the information is captured and displayed within a facility or complex the requirement is in the form many routers and switches.

(iii) Type of Information Transmitted

The transmission of ECG and simple video format from one point to another can be done through the analog telephone lines. However, the transmission of images and video conferencing system requires a high quality and high bandwidth telecommunication cable. It is also important to note that this information is sent in a compressed format, hence the requirement is more high-tech.

B. The Store and Forward Architecture

Here the transmission is intensive information package in the form of patient data, images, etc. The telephone lines which use analog, it means slow process and, therefore, more time for communication. The speed of transmission is an important factor in telemedicine technology and time constraints on the transfer of information must be given proper attention even in local area network. The following are the available connectivities in LAN:

(a) Regular Telephone Lines—with limited use.

(b) Local Area Networks:

  (i) Fibre optic/distributed data interface—rapid transmission, and

  (ii) Ethernet.

(c) Point to Point Copper T-1—High Bandwidth.

C. Network Termination Equipment (NTE)

NTE provides flow control, error checking, timing, signal enhancement and synchronisation of the information—audio, video and text—is converted into a electronic format by the acquisition equipment. NTE is not an integral part of the image and information acquisition equipment, but an inter-facility network for outside the network. This is a device where information from outside, i.e. other than the complex or campus of the institution, is received into the LAN. This is an additional requirement to extend inter-facility network to outside. This can be a poor man's Wide Area Network (WAN).

WIDE AREA NETWORK (WAN)

The Components and the factors of WAN Network:

(A) Bandwidth

(B) Telecommunication Carrier

(C) Distance of Transmission

(D) Real and Artificial Barrier for Transmission—(Geographical Barrier)

(E) Volume of Utilization

(F) Available Services

(G) Telecommunication Transmission Medium

(H) Image and Information Delivery/Display Equipment

(A) Bandwidth

The following factors are to be considered for requirement of bandwidth for telemedicine technology application:

(i) Store and Forward application is not time-sensitive and hence a low bandwidth and dial-up channel is sufficient in clinical practice. The bandwidth services with one ISDN line with 56 Kbps are most economical and practical. However, 3 lines are the real requirement in clinical application.

(ii) Real Time Application—This is extremely time-sensitive. This includes a video component and exchange of audio, video and images. A high bandwidth with at least three ISDN lines is an essential requirement for efficient transmission of data.

(iii) In location where transmission and exchange of

information between two centres is not very large and the video component is not included in the programme, POTS (Telephone) may be the most practical approach since this is most economical and readily available in rural and semi-urban programme. The transfer of data is, of course, slow and some of the resolutions may be lost during transmission. However, this can be one of the technologies, which can be used where ISDN lines are not available. In the Indian army, in the forward areas, this can be one of the ideal propositions for communication between the base and command hospitals and/or from the field hospitals.

(iv) In applications where large data is transmitted with full video conferencing system and video motion, telemedicine network requires very large bandwidth. The only option is fibre optic mediated services. The current ideal technology is 80 M (a synchronized transformer). These facilities have flexible bandwidth with dial-up strategy and are most economical and useful in large centres where the data is transmitted from many sources. However, these services are not readily available in many countries including India.

(B) Telecommunication Carrier

The telecommunication services at present are controlled by government and have several regulations operating in the country. The services in many parts, including large cities, do not include ISDN lines. Even in cities where ISDN lines are available the services are yet to be perfected. The present operations cost is also high. In due course private telecommunication providers are coming to India and the government has given clearance to the private operators, the services may become cost effective. In developed countries, the companies which were providing long distance services are now giving local exchange services as well and at a nominal cost and hence telemedicine application can be extended to the primacy centres and home-care environment. Slowly with the removal of regulatory restrictions and with emergence of private telecommunication companies in India, the telecommunication network will improve telemedicine application. They can also provide a turnkey solution to the Government and private organisations in health care delivery programme. These companies have potential advantages in that they can offer high bandwidth lines and also facilitate non-compressed high quality audio, video and data transmission.

(C) Distance of Transmission

It is a fact that the transmission of information from long distances is a costly affair. This is one of the components which is a pricing factor. The distance component can be a major factor in telemedicine practice and can be a determining factor in health care delivery. However, the best approach is the utilisation of satellite transmission facilities and we hope that a global satellite network with dial-up facilities with high bandwidth may be the available in future. This will be the most beneficial to telemedicine application in a developing country like India.

(D) Real and Artificial Barrier for Transmission—Geographical Barrier

Medicine is a State subject and this is applicable mostly in developed countries. Telemedicine network also has a geographical boundary in clinical practice. The main aim of telemedicine is to provide services to the community and it may cross the boundary of a State and even the country. This needs clarification and new regulations since consultation may be required from a referral hospital situated in other States or may be out of the country. This needs government approval for telemedicine application. The transmission of data can be a limiting factor from one country to other, if not from one State to another in a country like India.

In addition, the dense mountains ranges, forests and

isolated islands may limit the telemedicine services. In developed countries these factors have been overcome by building high microwave towers and repeaters (relay stations). The solution to laying down of cables may be most difficult in these areas and may be a high cost proposition.

(E) Volume of Utilisation

This factor depends upon the number of hours used for tele-consultation and transmission of data in a telemedicine network. The best way to express is:

Cost of dedicated line (per month =
Crossover point hour/month
Cost of switch services (per hour)

The dedicated or leased lines are only useful where the number of hours is fairly high and certainly the crossover point is higher; otherwise when the utilisation is fairly low the switch services like ISDN or even telephone line may be most practical. The cost of ISDN services is calculated as Rs. 500—1,500 per hour in India (depends on distance). This is besides the rental charges of Rs. 1,000 per month. This is certainly going to be down in future when more and more ISDN lines are brought in. In some of the countries, ISDN lines are recommended when the utilisation time is in the range of 100—150 hours per month. The leased lines are only recommended when the use is very high, at least 500 hours per month or so.

(F) Available Services

It is important to understand at this stage that many telecommunication services/facilities are not available in cities or semi-urban or rural areas. ISDN lines are not available in many areas at present and hence telephone services and/or satellite services in rural areas may be the only transmission media in telemedicine application. It is also important to know that satellite transmission is also not practical since it is costly and we hope in future the cost may be considerably reduced for its utilisation in these areas. We must understand right at the initial stage that telemedicine application has few options for telecommunication network. Although ISDN lines are most practical and economical in telemedicine application, the services are not readily available in many areas in India. Hopefully, these may be available in future especially with the emergence of private telecommunication network. Since we are to depend on telephone lines, our technology, including software and hardware, must be developed accordingly for transmission of audio, video and electronic patient record from one centre to another or to the referral hospital for consultation.

(G) Telecommunication Transmission

Medium

It is no doubt that fibre optic transmission is the best medium for telemedicine network. It is well understood that optical fibre at present not available in telemedicine application at a longer distance. It is only practical within a campus or in a city. We must use the digital microwave or digital satellite medium for transmission of data over long distances.

(H) Image and Information Delivery/Display Equipment

It is essential to know that as far as possible in telemedicine technology application, the sending and the receiving ends of the network should have identical acquisition and display equipment. This facilitates a better communication transmission and interpretation by the consultant/adviser. In interactive Real Time video conferencing telemedicine network, both ends of the connection essentially should have the same equipment. At both sides, the cameras and other devices for capturing information, microphones and mixtures for capturing audio input, must be the same. However, there can be differences in the number and size of the cameras and monitors but both ends should use the same basic components—2-way interactive Real-Time technology. In situations where one site is a primary and the other is a referral site or a consulting site, the consulting site may have more medical peripherals for acquisition and transmission of the information.

In Store and Forward telemedicine network, the referring site in teleradiology and telepathology practice should have a scanner, digital microscope and several digital-capture devices and a personal computer with software to manipulate the images and transmission of data. The receiving or the referral/consultant's end should be equipped with a high resolution monitor, display images and high capacity data archiving system to store all the received images (for a specified period of time). At the receiving site, there may not be a need for a scanner or digital-capture devices. However, this depends upon the availability of budget and as a matter of fact the receiving centre should also have all the facilities for digital-capture devices.

7

CHAPTER

Cyber Medicine

The networking of hospitals, clinics, rehabilitation centres and even private practice in some areas has opened new perspectives and possibilities of adaptation of working methodology within medical institutions and medical professionals. Personal computers are available to every professional and health care personnel and they can have access to the medical records of their patients with the emergence of modern hospital information system. This has made the professional colleagues at different hospitals exchange data and they can also use the powerful distributed data-base to get the necessary information via electronic net-communication. The process can help in better diagnosis and improved treatment techniques for the patients as well. All information transmission is done online or on offline with or without interaction facilities particularly synchronous, video conferencing and transmission of data where simple texts and images of the patients are transmitted from one location to another. This technology, which is feasible in health care today is generally called Cyber Medicine. The areas of Cyber Medicine can be discussed as follows:

1. Electronic Patient File,
2. Image and signal processing,
3. Graphic data-base,
4. Mobile data collection,
5. Visualizing of data,
6. Tele-teaching, and
7. Study telemedicine as an overview.

There have been great developments in Cyber Medicine in developed and western countries. The goals of India's cyber medicine can be discussed in the following format:

1. To provide medical information and resources that is specific to India.
2. To promote cross-fertilization of ideas between medical speciality areas.
3. To promote the use of computerised resources and cyber communication by medical professionals in India.
4. To provide an understanding of traditional and culture-based medical practices common to India.
5. To provide differentiation between evidence-based medicine, i.e. (allopathic) and culture-based medical practice especially for general public who might have access into cyber medicine as an authoritative medical source.

Cyber medicine in India can support and provide technical and required information in traditional and alternative medicine practiced particularly in Ayurvedic, Homeopathy and Unani, which are quite prevalent in India. The professionals and also the general public have not given adequate information and knowledge about the culture-based medicine in Indian scene. They are still practised by persons who have no training in general medicine, which includes the disease-process and their effects on the body and organs. These practioners do not have adequate information about anatomy, physiology, pathology and pharmacology and their practice is mainly directed to the patients based on their narration in front of the so-called medical doctor. All the medical professionals including specialists and super-specialists should be given adequate information and these traditional medicines should be defined along with their techniques through cyber medicine programme. There is no doubt that Indian Medical portal information is currently virtually explored into a number of cities that are available for professionals as well as to the public. We have found that not all the specialities are always covered. Many features are incomplete and not everything works smoothly in spite of the modern developments and technology in the world. However, some of the portals I have found show a lot of promise and certainly they can improve in their working and technical information. There are several medical associations and so-cities in India. Many of them have started to put up their own web pages. You can now get information on these organisations, their activities, membership guidelines and procedures from these websites. It is certainly encouraging. However, it would be better if they put up more scientific contents on their cities so that they could become sources of useful information to our own scientists, medical professionals and para-medical professionals including nurses.

The number of medical colleges in India have information and functional websites. They regularly update information and functional websites. They regularly update information and other news for instant access to the professionals and related scientists. The AIIMS, New Delhi and PGI, Chandigarh have their most informative and functional websites and are being used mainly by the professionals. MCI and NBE have their own websites and they are also being used for detailed information and for the post-graduate entrance examinations as well. However, the scientific content and the development of medical technology are somewhat missing except in some websites, which give case reports and other experience-sharing process to the professionals as educational material for improving their knowledge. It is also essential to know that the research areas are greatly missing in these sites. There are also a few cyber lectures and useful links of medical professionals. Indmedica has initiated a programme in association with some professionals and provides speciality news and even cyber lectures and also supports links to other medical websites and professionals. The Indian doctors' network "Online Health India" Meditimes have very useful links to Indian and international medical sites and professionals. They have also features and fora for discussion between doctors and medical clubs for advice among their colleagues. The sites also have some access to the journals and conference notices for the ready information for the professionals. "Doctor Anywhere" who have started their programme with a bang and was particularly focused on "Doctor-to-doctor consultation" service where a non-specialist doctor can consult a specialist consultant on a case-to-case basis. They have also additional facilities for online messages and chats. In this cyber medicine programme investigation reports and images can also be sent online to the consultants. The service relates that a referring doctor pays the consultant for his services a consulting fee through the Doctor Anywhere portal service. Both the referring and the consultant doctors have to register with the portal with a fee for using their portals. This was the best portal service where a general practioners sitting in any corner of the country can take advice of the specialists and super-specialists from any corner of India with certainly a very small amount and certainly much less than the travel cost and time required for the travel of the patients and their relations. The portal and services, however, which were used greatly in the past has now fallen into a low practice area. The portal is no longer economically advantageous. This is a great loss to the medical fraternity. The portal also developed a very simple electronic patient data with images at a very nominal cost. We were involved in the beginning of this group at programme and have really given all the supports and also saved many prestigious lives by consultation provided by the specialists and super-specialists of PGI, Chandigarh practically free of cost to the general practioners. We should see that this kind of portals or even

Doctor Anywhere sites should be viewed by the government and semi-government organisations and they can be given a new life for the best utilisation of cyber medicine.

The future development should include all aspects particularly tele-care, tele-health, tele-education and in true practice of telemedicine in future. We should also see that health care workers who have practically no access to modern development and medical practice should also get the information by using the portals.

We should see that more and more medical problems and discussions should take place even at a distance for some disciplines such as tele-radiology, tele-dermatology and tele-pathology that are already developed to a substantial extent. With time, this needs expansion with other disciplines especially psychiatry, mother and child clinics, and general medical practice. The relationships between patients and health personnel should take place in virtual medical practice. We hope that during this time consultations and new kinds of information will be available including 3-Dimensional representations of the body, tactile stimuli and smell power can be developed gradually. We fee that it is also likely that technological advances will permit more treatment to be performed at a distance. We hope that in future the health workers posted in rural clinics will probably be connected to the network including the mobile telephone and we desire that video conferencing facilities be extended to village or community health centre with district and teaching hospitals.

Similarly, we desire and the technology will certainly permit the patient's perspective. It should be possible to receive medical care whenever and wherever it is requested. The patients in future will not be dependent upon their own doctor only. They can make the right choice. This can fulfil the need for other professionals and will certainly have the individual's choice, the most appropriate health services depending upon a particular problem or area of concern.

RELEVANCE OF CYBER MEDICINE IN DEVELOPING COUNTRIES—PARTICULARLY THE ONE LIKE INDIA

"Health for all by 2000" can be partially met by using cyber medicine through portals and telemedicine technology. The slogan is feasible through the recent developments make it relevant even today that we are committed to provide evenly health care to our people. Every citizen should have access to appropriate medical professionals and specialists for medical consultation. It is a fact of life that all men are equal and should be given priority in medical consultation and health care. We should realise that we are not able to provide total primary medical care in the rural and semi-urban areas. Secondary and tertiary medical care is not uniformally available in urban and semi-urban areas except in metropolitan and some of the major cities in India. This creates professional isolation which is not ideal for the profession and certainly leads to mediocrity. We should realise and it is a phenomenon that computer literacy is fast developing in the urban and semi-urban areas in our country and this can be extended to the rural areas as well where the requisite communication infrastructure is now available. It is easier to set-up excellent tele-communication infrastructure in semi-urban or rural India than to place thousands of medical specialists in these places which is certainly not feasible due to shortage of specialists and who are not readily available.

Telemedicine with satellite-based technology is now available and ISRO is providing the connectivity with minimal or even free of cost in health care sector. This is indeed a great service that the satellite system will soon be available for communication and utilisation of connectivity with our primary and secondary care hospitals. We should take the advantages of the phenomenal explosion in the use of computers in many parts of the country especially urban, semi-urban and rural areas.

Major hospitals and institutions can extend their skills to the remote primary and secondary centres. The distance becomes immaterial. Health care information, preventive vaccination programmes, providing information for expectant mothers, information about specific diseases, etc. can be universally available by using cyber medicine and through the material inserted by the specialists in the portals.

We have seen the Information Technology has changed and will continue to change the health care delivery in Western and other developed countries. We have also seen and witnessed a growth in technology unprecedented in the annals of history. The technology—particularly telemedicine and cyber medicine—has not made a significant impact on the main stream medicine in India even though IT revolution was started from this country and manpower is produced in a large number and they are occupying important positions in every part of the world. The development of software is a great industry and comprises sizeable earning in foreign exchange and job opportunities to the Indian technologist and scientists. We should see that at least the younger generation in medical profession should utilise the technology for providing greater support to the patients and to give their best in health care delivery system. We shall accept the challenge and the considerable scope for improvement in clinical practice of medicine. We should know where and how to implement which technology and at what cost available to us. Use of portals and cyber medicine and also telemedicine technology in transmission of data from one location to another can be powerful tool for young doctors and professionals. We should see that the future is promising to be excited. The junior hospital staff that has considerable limitations can have access to and have communication links with the senior consultants, which will help in taking correct decisions in diagnosis and treatment. Now by using the information technology, the patient need not wait for next day or for days for his/her treatment. We should see that we make use of the indigenous technology, which has been developed and is in developing phase. We can practice modern medicine with expert advice of eminent physicians and surgeons and specialists from India and in case there is a need from abroad. We should see that we use the modern technology for online and offline transmission of ECG, Images, pathology reports and even doctors' prescriptions for patient welfare and for best line of treatment. The specialists too can get a second opinion promptly. Radiology and Pathology centres will interact electronically and give their expert opinion in specialities like accidents, medicine and dermatology which process will allow the specialists to interact with primary physician and/or with the patients if the portals is available and open for the patients. Workstations with necessary software will be a common feature in the homes of the specialists. Like any other professionals, the tele-specialists of the future will offer advice from the comfort of his clinic or even home without having to travel long distances. There are many online medical and general subjects' data-base on the web that need to be focused for general practioners, specialists and super-specialists, medical professionals practising in India. They have enormous information on tele-health, tele-radiology and other related subjects, which can be most useful as distance learning resource facilities. There are several discussion groups and also list-serves all available as e-mail forum. Professionals as well as non-professionals can exchange information by using internet services on virtually any subject. One can either register as a member of the forum or list-serve to receive all information and also request for more information on the subject of their own choice. At present, there are thousands of list-serves each devoted to a particular topic. One site which catalogues them in catalyst is one of the commonly used by professionals including medical. The list-serves can be further moderated especially in e-mail posted to the members or the forum goes first to a moderator who decides where the posting of lectures or information is appropriate for all members.

The list-serves can be a double-edged sword. On the one hand, they can be a valuable source of information or a way to get a question answered quickly by someone who has already solved a similar problem. On the other, subscribers can be loaded by several postings a day many of which may be of no interest at all. Many other forums operate and digest the operation where you can receive all messages once a week or a month and you can channelise in one sitting only. We should understand that the discussion groups or the forum are similar to the old computer bulletin boards where you long into a site to join a discussion or post a question. Most are available these days via web browsers. Indmedica which has designed and perhaps one of the first cyber-medicine portal is providing one of the useful fora to medical professionals in general and eye specialists in particular. Any interesting subject or case discussion or even a clinical material is posted in their website for the user-member. The best thing in this portal is that the moderator sits at one end and he is the person to channelise and direct the interesting material for the user.

In this Chapter we are trying to develop the technology of how to use cyber medicine as a portal for medical practice and future medicine programme. We will also try to discuss the technological advances and requirements including the organizational changes that are necessary for the greater use of these portals by our medical professionals in India. We feel that the future—the time period being up to 2010 where we can achieve the goal that each and every professional and other para-medical and nursing professionals can be benefited by the portals. Our aim should be that this can offer the means by which access to health care and health-related information can be provided to all concerned. Our attempts should also be that the beneficiaries of such increased access to cyber medicine are likely to extend to the students and certainly to the public at large.

EXPANSION AND SCOPE OF INDIA'S CYBER MEDICINE

1. To provide medical information and sources that is specific to India.
2. To promote discussion and close cooperation and exchange of ideas between medical specialists and super-specialists.
3. To promote the use of computer resources and cyber communication by medical professionals in India.
4. To provide the knowledge and understanding of

the traditional and culture-based medical practice, particularly the Ayurveda and Homoeopathy, to the medical professionals in India. This is an important area since the traditional medicines have considerably improved and they continue to develop on scientific lines especially with greater emphasis on formulations. The information is urgently needed to the medical professionals for their greater information and understanding. Also it is important to know that practically no significant research has been undertaken to make a comparative study or to demarcate the diseases where singly or in combination these systems can produce better results.

5. To provide differentiation between evidence-based medicine and culture-based medical practices especially for the general practioners to get the knowledge.

We must know that traditional and alternative medical practices, particularly the Ayurveda, Homoeopathy and Unani, are quite prevalent in India. It is essential and important that there should be well-defined processes in these areas for disseminating information to very practioner in the country. Cyber Medicine can be one of the areas where these can be utilised. We must clearly understand that alternative medicines have a strong presence in India and these should be given proper and adequate representation in the cyber medicine programme.

TELEMEDICINE FROM THE PATIENT'S PERSPECTIVE

The global availability and access to health care is likely to result in a complete restructuring of how medical care is to be delivered in future. A country like India, which has joined the globalization process in their development programme, will also join hands in health care sector as well. Telemedicine technology and distance medicine can be one of the useful media in health care institutions in monitoring and treating individuals in their own environment with direct and indirect access to the global medical programme. We are sure that the health institutions in India, government as well as private, will be able to make use of Telemedicine to share their personnel and take help from the experts from any part of the national and international fields who can support the diagnosis and treatment of the deserving patients. In future for Telemedicine application, it will not be necessary for the hospitals, particularly private institutions, to have all the experts in medical fields within their premises which will be quite expensive. They need not attached to one centre and avoiding huge cost involved in keeping them within their hospitals/ institutions. These institutions will be able to share the cost and expenses by having an expert from one institution covering a number of hospitals at distances who can support the management and health care delivery to their patients. We must also remember that in certain situations, telemedicine practice has the potential to improve health care delivery by permitting Centralisation of specialists' expertise, which is certainly very efficient, and this can make it possible to disseminate such expertise beyond the centre or city and need not remain confined to a geographical location.

The patients can be the greatest beneficiaries by the recent developments by internet access and now even the remotest villages and semi-urban areas will at least be aware of the possibility of health care delivery and will choose the right approach for their ailments and can also discuss with the available medical professionals on the alternate information/ opinion thus available through the portals and health care programme. We must not think that this can be a demanding by the patients and it will create an atmosphere of challenging the experience and authority of local medical professionals. We feel that the health care delivery should be available to everyone everywhere and at all times of need and the information is accessible to the people as well. We should see that telemedicine in patient care should be used as a means of augmenting health care and will not reflect the evaluation on the part of medical professionals stationed in those areas. It should not be mis-interpreted and should necessarily distinguish from the normal medical practice and should not be treated as something new in clinical practice. The local medical professionals certainly should remain the main focus of interest in the diagnosis and treatment of patients and it should not be regarded as interference but only as a medium for discussion and experience-sharing for the improvement in the patient care.

Glossary

1. Algorithm

A mathematical coding scheme for compressing digitised broadband video or audio signals so that the signals can be transmitted over a lower bandwidth.

2. Analog

Information (electronic or otherwise) that is created and transmitted as a continuous stream. Compare this to digital information generated by computers. Modems are used to convert digital computer data to analog form for sending over standard POTS lines.

3. ATM : Asynchronous Transfer Mode

A telecommunications service that supports switched multimedia communication from T1 (1.544 Mbps) to very high data rates (155 Mbps and higher).

4. Bandwidth

The capacity of an electronic transmission medium to transmit data per unit of time. The higher the bandwidth, the more data can be transmitted. Typically measured in kilobytes or megabytes per second (Kbps, Mbps). Standard telephones are low bandwidth devices (maximum bandwidth = 33.6 Kbps). Cable television uses high bandwidth (up to 140 Mbps).

5. Bit : Binary Digit

The basic 0-1 unit of information used by computers for information entry, storage and transmission. Data rates in telecommunications are often referred to in bits (abbreviated 'b') per second.

6. Byte

Each data character, such as the letter A, is composed of 8 bits, called a "byte" (abbreviated "B"). Units of storage are often referred to in terms of the number of bytes (e.g., a "100 MB hard drive").

7. CCD

Charge coupled device = "chip". A 1-CCD (1-"chip") camera contains a single charge coupled device with specialised semi-conductors. These contain photo-sensitive cells that generate voltage when struck by photons of light. One photosensitive cell equates to one pixel in the displayed image. Three chip cameras 3-CCD provide images with high resolution and better colour representation, and can cost ten times as much as 1-CCD cameras.

8. CODEC

Coder/Decoder (also Compression/Decompression) hardware and/or software used with interactive video systems that converts an analog signal to digital, then compresses it so that lower bandwidth tele-communication lines can be used.

9. Database

Information consisting of many parts or units set out in an organized way, such as in a list, chart or table. Databases can be soften, updated or manipulated in various ways. For example, using a computer database about students in a school, you could list their names by alphatical order, by age, even by weight or height.

10. DICOM: Digital Imaging and Communications in Medicine

An industry standard for connection of, and communication among, medical imaging devices. The most recent iteration is DICOM 3.

11. Digital

Information coded in discrete numeral values (bits). Digital data streams are less susceptible to interference than analog data streams. Also because they are made up of zeros and ones (bits) than can be manipulated and integrated easily with other data streams (voice/video/data).

12. Digital Camera

Captures images (still or motion) digitally and does not require analog-to-digital conversion before the image can be transmitted or stored in a computer.

13. Frame Rate Frames Per Second (fps)

Displayed on a video monitor. A frame rate of 25-30 fps is considered "full motion" and is what most broadcast video operates at. A frame rate of 15 fps is noticeably 'jerky'.

14. Gray Scale

The levels (shades) of gray that a screen or pixel within a screen can display.

15. HIS : Hospital Information System

One that supports all hospital functions and activities such as patient records, scheduling, administration, charge-back and billing, and often links to or includes clinical information systems such as an RIS.

16. HL7 : Health Level 7

A standard interface between hospital information

systems. The HL7 standard defines the format for interchange of text files between healthcare databases.

17. HTML : Hyper Text Markup Language

A simple computer language used for formatting and presentation of Internet hyper-media documents. It is used to embed hypertext links ("hot links") into documents.

18. Image Management

Stored image management denotes the ability to sort, arrange, and manipulate stored images into functional groups.

19. Interface

How the system enables information to be accessed and modified. A graphical user interface (GUI) is typically simple to use, with more controlled point-and-click on screen icons.

20. Internet

A loose aggregation of thousands of computer networks forming an enormous worldwide.

21. ISDN : Integrated Services Digital Network

A low-to-medium speed technology for digital telephony. Usually transmits at 64—128 Kbps, although higher speeds are possible. ISDN is broken into 64 Kbps bearer channels (B-channels) and 16 Kbps data channels (D-channels). Basic Rate Interface (BRI) generally provides a 128 Kbps data rate ("2B+D"), while Primary Rate Interface (BRI) can provide up to 1.54 Maps (the equivalent of a TI circuit).

22. ISP : Internet Service Provider

The local, regional or national (VSNL) Company that provides dial-up connections to the Internet, as well as hosting of home pages.

23. JPEG : Joint Photographic Experts Group

This international group, a joint efforts of the ISO (International Standardisation Organisation) has developed standards for still images compression. Motion JPEG applied JPEG compression to each frame of a video clip.

24. Kbps

Kilobytes (thousands of bits) per second. A typical compressed video clinical interaction is transmitted at 385 Kbps.

25. LAN : Local Area Network

A computer network linking computers, printers, servers, and other equipment within a campus. Can support audio, video, and data exchange.

26. Laser Digitizer

Laser scanner, Employs a laser to capture image information to digital form. Very high resolution and wide gray scale range are possible. Because it uses coherent light, the laser scanner can penetrate thick films (an ability measured in units of optical density).

27. Leased Line

Private line, a point-to-point connection that is logically similar to two cans tied together with a dedicated piece of string. You pay for the sole use of the circuit and the price does not vary as a function of usage, as with switched lines.

28. Mbps

Megabytes (millions of bits) per second. A typical uncompressed video signal requires 45 Mbps (or more) to transmit.

29. Modem: Modulator/Demodulator

Enables transmission of digital data (by transforming it to and from analog waveforms) over standard analog phone lines and cable video systems.

30. PACS : Picture Archiving and Communication System

An image system that embraces all modalities (X-ray, CT, MR, nuclear medicine, ultrasound) and links users with display work-stations over a high speed network to an image server, an archive, printers and radiology information systems.

31. Pixel

The smallest unit of raster display. A picture cell with specific color and/or brightness. The more pixels an image has, the more detail, or resolution, it can display. The pixel size in a high-end computer monitor's screen (a "1K x 1K monitor") is approximately 0.28 x 0.28 mm. The pixel size for diagnostic tele-radiology monitors ("2K x 2K") is much smaller than this.

32. POTS: Plain Old Telephone System

The analog, public switched telephone network in common use throughout the world. Also known as Public Switched Telephone Network (PSTN). Enables voice phone calls and data transmission of up to 33.6 Kbps.

33. Real Time

Sends and receives audio/video/data simultaneously, without more than a fraction of a second delay. Applications that are transmitted within a few seconds are sometimes called nearer real time.

34. Resolution

The level of detail that can be captured or displayed. For video displays (Teleradiology or interactive video) resolution is measured in pixels x lines x bit depth.

35. RAM : Random Access Memory

Information that can be stored, recalled and updated in an instant.

36. ROM : Read-Only Memory

Information that is stored in a computer's ROM microchips. It can be detected, or read, but it cannot be altered or rewritten. It does not disappear when the computer is switched off.

37. Router

A device which routes data to the segment of the network it was meant to go to, rather than be broadcast to all segments.

38. Store-and-Forward

Captured audio clips, video clips, still images, or data that is transmitted or received at a later time (sometimes no more than a minute). Enables dis-synchronous communication, with the advantage of not needing concurrent participant involvement.

39. Switched Line or Network

A telecommunications option that operates like a dial-up phone line (which is, in fact, a switched line-as are ISDN, ATM, switched 56). There is often a usage charge for switched services, particularly for long distance connections such as phone lines.

40. Telecommunications

Sending-receiving or communicating information over long distances, such as between computers or telephones.

Telecommunication systems use metal wires, fibre-optic cables, radio signals, satellite links and other methods.

41. Twisted Pair

A pair of copper wires that have been twisted to minimize electronic interference. Standard phone wire.

42. URL: Universal Resource Locator

The World Wide Web address (typically in the form : http:www.name-of-site) of an Internet home page or other document.

43. Virtual Reality

An object, scene, landscape or something similar which seems real to our senses, but is not because it is created by a computer.

44. WAN : Wide Area Network

Wider in geographic scope than a LAN. Provides digital communications (voice/video/data) over switched (ISDN, switched 56) or unswitched (fractional T1, T1) networks.

45. Wavelets

An image compression technique that enables more or less loss less compression ratios of 10:1 or even 20:1, compared to the standard 3:1 maximum for loss less JPEG compression.

Bibliography

Allen, A. and Wheeler, T.: The leaders: US programs doing more than 500 interactive consults in 1997. *Telemedicine Today,* 1998:6(3) 36-37.

Brahams, D.: The medico legal implications of tele-consulting in the UK. *Journal of Telemedicine and Telecare,* 1995:1:196-201.

Darkins, A.: The management of clinical risk in telemedicine application. *Journal of Telemedicine and Telecare.* 1996:2: 179-184.

Darkins, A., Dearden, C.H., Rocke, L.G., Martin, J.B., Sibson, L. and Wootton, R.: An evaluation of telemedical support for minor treatment centre. *Journal of Telemedicine and Telecare,* 1996:2:93-99.

Doolittle, G.C. and Allen, A.: Practising Oncology via telemedicine. *Journal of Telemedicine and Telecare,* 1997: 3: 335-343.

Friedman, R.H., Kazis, L.E. and Jette, A. *et al.* A telecommunication system for monitoring and Counselling patients with hypertension. *American Journal of Hypertension,* 1999: 9: 285-292.

Harrison, R., Clayton, W. and Wallace, P.: Can telemedicine be used to improve communication between primary and secondary care. *BMJ,* 1996: 313: 1377-1381.

Hawker, F., Kavanagh, S., Yellowheels, P. and Kalucy, R.S.: Telepsychiatry in South Australia. *Journal of Telemedicine and Telecare*, 1998:4:187-194.

Loan, M.S., Corbett, R. and Bloomer, S.E. *et al.*: Diagnostic accuracy and clinical management by real time Teledermatology. Results from the Northern Ireland arms of the UK Multicentre Teledermatology trial. *Journal of Telemedicine and Telecare*, 1998: 4: 95-100.

McCue, M.J., Maxman, P.E. and Hampton, C. *et al.* The case of Powhatan Correctional Centre/Virginia Department of Corrections and Virginia Commonwealth University/ Medical College of Virginia. *Telemedicine Journal*, 1997: 3:11-17.

Satava, R.M.: Virtual reality and telepresence for military medicine. *Computers in Biology and Medicine*, 1995: 25:229-236.

Smith, R.: The future of health care systems. *BMJ*, 1997: 31 2:1495-1496.

Stromer, J., Bolle, S.R. and Sund, T. 1: ROC study of a Teleradiology workstation *versus* film reading. *Acta Radiologica*, 1997: 38:176-180.

Taylor, P.: A survey of research in telemedicine 1: Telemedicine systems. *Journal of Telemedicine and Telecare*, 1998:4:1-17.

Treister, N.W.: Physician acceptance of new medical information systems. The field of dreams. *Physician Executive*, 1998: May/June: 20-24.

Whitten, P., Cook, D.J. and Shaw, P. *et al.*: Telekidcare: bringing health care into schools. *Telemedicine Journal*, 1999:4:335-342.

Whitten, P. and Franken, E.A.: Telemedicine for patient consultation: factors affecting use by rural primary care physicians in Kansas. *Journal of Telemedicine and Telecare,* 1995:1:139-144.

Yellowlees, P.: Successful development of telemedicine systems—seven core principles. *Journal of Telemedicine and Telecare,* 1997:3: 25-222.

Young, H.L.: Satellite-delivered medical education and training for central Europe: a TEMPUS project. *Journal of Telemedicine and Telecare,* 1996:2:14-19.

Index